T0100239

Roguelike Development with JavaScript

Build and Publish Roguelike Genre Games with JavaScript and Phaser

Andre Alves Garzia

Apress®

Roguelike Development with JavaScript: Build and Publish Roguelike Genre Games with JavaScript and Phaser

Andre Alves Garzia
London, UK

ISBN-13 (pbk): 978-1-4842-6058-6   ISBN-13 (electronic): 978-1-4842-6059-3
https://doi.org/10.1007/978-1-4842-6059-3

Managing Director, Apress Media LLC: Welmoed Spahr
Acquisitions Editor: Spandana Chatterjee
Development Editor: Matthew Moodie
Coordinating Editor: Divya Modi

Cover designed by eStudioCalamar

Cover image designed by Pixabay

Distributed to the book trade worldwide by Springer Science+Business Media New York, 233 Spring Street, 6th Floor, New York, NY 10013. Phone 1-800-SPRINGER, fax (201) 348-4505, e-mail orders-ny@springer-sbm.com, or visit www.springeronline.com. Apress Media, LLC is a California LLC and the sole member (owner) is Springer Science + Business Media Finance Inc (SSBM Finance Inc). SSBM Finance Inc is a **Delaware** corporation.

For information on translations, please e-mail booktranslations@springernature.com; for reprint, paperback, or audio rights, please e-mail bookpermissions@springernature.com.

Apress titles may be purchased in bulk for academic, corporate, or promotional use. eBook versions and licenses are also available for most titles. For more information, reference our Print and eBook Bulk Sales web page at http://www.apress.com/bulk-sales.

Any source code or other supplementary material referenced by the author in this book is available to readers on GitHub via the book's product page, located at www.apress.com/978-1-4842-6058-6. For more detailed information, please visit http://www.apress.com/source-code.

Printed on acid-free paper

To Lily, Cleo, and Alfafa, who I kept awake by typing throughout the night.

Table of Contents

About the Author

Andre Alves Garzia is a developer who loves web and game development. In recent years, he has published books about building games for Firefox OS and managed a web literacy program in vulnerable neighborhoods of Rio de Janeiro. He is a firm believer in empowerment through technological experimentation and thinks game development should be on everyone's bucket list. He lives in London and wonders if the UK procedural generator is biased toward raining.

About the Technical Reviewer

Cédric Stoquer has been in the video game industry for more than 10 years, as a JavaScript game and engine developer. He worked on projects for Ankama, Square Enix, and Bandai Namco. He is the creator of *Pixelbox*, an all-in-one 2D game engine for making retro-looking games with JavaScript. Cédric can be found on Twitter at @cstoquer or reached at https://cstoquer.itch.io/pixelbox.

Acknowledgments

This author holds a debt of gratitude to all the amazing people who, decade after decade, keep producing amazing roguelike content and making it freely available online. To the welcoming warmth of communities like RogueBasin,[1] Roguelike Celebration,[2] and the roguelikedev[3] subreddit, without their content I wouldn't know where to start.

To Kenney,[4] who is an eternal fountain of generosity and makes a ton of free game assets. Their 1-Bit Pack is used in this book and is responsible for most of the charm you'll see on screen.

To Jack Oatley,[5] who made the Doomed font which we use in Chapter 9. That font is sick!

To Xueqiao Xu,[6] whose pathfinding library is at the heart of all that is dangerous inside our dungeon.

To Richard Davies and the team behind Phaser,[7] my dream library to work web games.

To Andrzej Mazur,[8] who keeps inspiring me to create gamedev content since all the way back to the old Firefox OS days.

And finally to the editorial team at Apress, who were patient and helpful amid an ever-changing world.

---

[1] www.roguebasin.com/index.php?title=Main_Page

[2] https://roguelike.club/

[3] www.reddit.com/r/roguelikedev/

[4] https://kenney.nl/

[5] http://jack-oatley.com/

[6] http://xueqiaoxu.me/

[7] https://phaser.io/

[8] https://end3r.com/

Introduction

Before anything else, thank you for your purchase; without curious readers like you, this book has no reason for existing. I am excited to be joining you on a game development journey through the chapters of this book and beyond. Together, we'll develop a casual roguelike game based on web technologies and learn more about this beloved and enduring genre.

By the end of the book, you'll have a toolset and a game that can be used to build more complex and rewarding roguelike experiences; you'll also have a collection of links and resources to investigate and learn more about both general game development and specific roguelike techniques.

Who this book is for

This book is intended for web developers and web game developers who are curious about roguelikes. You don't need to be a JavaScript ninja to be able to handle the code in this book; I have kept the code simple and flexible so that beginners and intermediate developers can feel confident not only to understand what is on the source files but also to tweak them to their hearts' content.

If you are already a roguelike developer but have been working with a different language and are curious about web technologies, this book will be a rewarding experience for you. Some of the roguelike techniques shown will feel basic for seasoned roguelike developers; just remember that this is an introductory book, and the first steps in any journey are usually the easiest ones, and that taking these initial steps is necessary for newcomers to the genre.

How to approach this book

I'm a firm believer in technological experiments, so I have organized the chapters and the code for this book to be approachable and inviting to tinkerers and curious minds. The best way to approach each chapter is first to read and understand the examples presented in it and then play, mold, craft, tweak, and experiment a lot with it before moving to the next chapter.

The examples that we'll build are a bit vanilla; they lack what makes a game your game. By changing the code and taking ownership over it, you'll craft something that is uniquely yours, and that is always more rewarding than whatever example I could build.

Our approach is one of working and reworking through the code as we move through chapters and build more complex features. Like any roguelike game, we'll reach dead ends, backtrack, find and squash bugs. This is not about presenting a pristine single sample from which you could grasp the true nature of roguelike development; instead it is about building incrementally, having fun as we learn, and iterating as our ideas and knowledge evolve. No game is developed perfectly from the start; all games go through iterations, and so do our samples.

Your journey starts when you turn the next page.

CHAPTER 1

Before We Begin

What are roguelikes?

Welcome to the beginning of your game development journey, dear
reader; together we're going to work through many chapters as we build a
casual roguelike game. But before diving deep into that, we should spend
some time defining and contextualizing what are roguelike games, where
they come from, and what is the definition we are going to use to define
this genre in this book.

The one thing most people agree is that it all started with a game called
Rogue created in the early 1980s. This game combined early influences
from the 1970s such as *Colossal Cave Adventure*, which was a text-based
adventure game that made use of interactive fiction to present textual
descriptions of the scenes and collect text input about actions, and the
gameplay of a pen and paper role-playing game like *Dungeons & Dragons*,
in which players explore a dungeon filled with monsters and treasure.
What *Rogue* brought to the table was a spatial representation of the game
by drawing the game world onto the screen using ASCII characters (as can
be seen in Figure 1-1), instead of describing it using natural language, and
infinite replayability by using random generation to produce the mazes
and dungeons. A game of *Rogue* was always a unique experience; you
could play it over and over.

© Andre Alves Garzia 2020
A. A. Garzia, *Roguelike Development with JavaScript*,
https://doi.org/10.1007/978-1-4842-6059-3_1

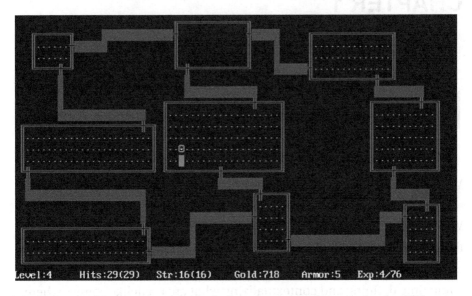

Figure 1-1. *A representation of what a game of Rogue looked like in an IBM PC[1]*

From that period onward, there were hundreds of roguelike games released. Roguelike is one of the few gaming genres from the 1980s that is still popular and seeing constant fresh releases and innovation. The problem with long-lived genres is that they end up amassing such a large corpus of content that it becomes really hard to define them. The roguelike community still has its fair share of flame wars trying to decide if one game is a roguelike or not. Be aware that many features we take as the staples of the genre were not present in the early days and that those early developers didn't care if their game was a roguelike or not; all they wanted to do was to ship good games. In due time, many of those games converged toward a common set of features which became cornerstones of the genre.

---

[1]Image by Michael Toy, Kenneth C.R.C. Arnold, Jo. Released in the public domain.

The Berlin Interpretation

In 2008, people present at the International Roguelike Development Conference coined what became known as *The Berlin Interpretation*[2] which is an attempt at defining what a roguelike is. They decided upon a canon of games, and the definition of *what is a roguelike* was extracted from the common set of features present in those games. The games in the canon were *Rogue, NetHack, Angband,* and *ADOM.* From that set of features, they further divided them into *high-value factors* and *low-value factors,* which can be viewed in Tables 1-1 and 1-2. A game doesn't need to have all those factors to be a roguelike, but this list helps us understand what this community valued at that time and place.

Table 1-1. *High-value factors in roguelikes according to The Berlin Interpretation*

Factor	Explanation
Random generation	The world is randomly generated so that each game is unique.
Permadeath	Dying in the game causes it to start over from the beginning.
Turn based	The game reacts after the user input. The player can wait and plan their move without fear that things are happening behind their back.
Grid based	The game is represented in a grid; both the players and all the other game entities (such as enemies) are placed on this grid.

(continued)

---

[2]www.roguebasin.com/index.php?title=Berlin_Interpretation

Table 1-1. (*continued*)

Factor	Explanation
Nonmodal	All the actions that are possible in the game are possible on the same screen. There is no need to switch to different modes of play.
Complexity	The game is complex and flexible enough to allow multiple solutions for the challenges presented during gameplay.
Resource management	In-game resources are limited, and managing them is part of the fun.
Hack'n'slash	Killing lots of enemies is part of the game.
Exploration and discovery	The game requires the player to explore through different levels and discover mysterious objects and entities and their interplay.

Even in the selected canon of games, those factors are not always present. Both *Angband* and *ADOM* have different modes, for example.

Table 1-2. *Low-value factors in roguelikes according to The Berlin Interpretation*

Factor	Explanation
Single player character	The game is focused on the player controlling a single character throughout the gameplay.
Enemies and players are similar	The mechanisms and features that apply to players also apply to enemies.
Tactical challenge	It is crucial to learn tactics to complete the game. Due to the procedural generation, you can't simply memorize how to win.

(*continued*)

Table 1-2. (*continued*)

Factor	Explanation
ASCII display	It is customary for roguelikes to use ASCII to build its interface.
Dungeons	Most roguelikes are dungeon based with multiple levels, mazes, and rooms.
Numbers	The values used to represent character characteristics and traits are deliberately shown.

There are many criticisms of The Berlin Interpretation. Many people feel that the definition is dated and not representative of the current state of roguelikes.[3] I've included it in this book to help us think about these factors and which of them are valuable to us. The categorization of games into an ever-evolving genre is quite difficult, and I don't believe we should spend too much time worrying if we're roguelike enough to merit the moniker in the little game we'll build together through the course of this book.

What are roguelites?

Diving deeper into the mud of categorization, there is another label we need to learn about even if only to reject it later: roguelites. The usual roguelike is a game that rewards investment of time and study. To ascend in a game such as *NetHack*, you'll need to invest a lot of time learning tactics and features and be prepared to play it over and over again. A game such as *Dwarf Fortress*, a fantastic game that by many dated categorization

---

[3]"Screw the Berlin Interpretation!" article: www.gamesofgrey.com/blog/?p=403

schemes would barely qualify as a roguelike but that in my own opinion is indeed a superb roguelike, is a game that is almost impossible to play effectively without its wiki and the associated community articles about it.

As you might have guessed, there is a whole niche of casual gamers that was not being served by the usual roguelikes. With the advent of smartphones and other small mobile computing devices, there was a surge in casual gaming. People want to game in their commutes. *Pick up and play* games that are quick and don't require a huge investment before you're having fun are the most common released games these days. Roguelites are the answer to that need. They are games that are easy to pick up and play without the need of learning complex mechanisms. They often skew toward fully graphical interfaces with less possible actions than the more traditional roguelikes and are very popular.

The problem with all the categorization is where you draw the line. What extra feature do you add to a roguelite that makes it spill over and become a roguelike? Is it even worth making such distinction? Those are rhetorical questions that the community is still heavily invested in debating. This kind of simpler roguelike has been known by other labels such as *roguelike-like*, *roguelike-ish*, and so on. It doesn't really matter. What is important is that some people want to make it possible to distinguish when a roguelike game is simpler and caters toward casual gaming.

What are roguelikes for this book?

For this book, we're defining a roguelike as a game that

- Uses procedural generation to produce its tile-based world

- Has permadeath

- Uses a turn-based action system

- Has multiple levels for the player to explore

Why develop roguelikes?

Game development in general is not only fun but it teaches you many techniques and approaches to common programming challenges that are applicable way beyond gaming. Roguelikes in particular will appeal to those who enjoy computer science, for it allows them to focus on algorithms, data structures, and their interactions. It will also be a wonderful medium for those of us who enjoy storytelling and worldbuilding, for a roguelike lives and dies by the sum of its mechanics, themes, and gameplay. In essence, roguelikes will provide a rich and engaging platform for both sides of your brain. There is a lot for your analytical side to ponder upon and experiment with and even more for your creative side to craft and give life.

Roguelikes are among the few gaming genres where solo developers and small teams are not at a huge disadvantage against major studios. Your roguelike can make a mark in the industry and be loved by its players and other developers alike. The roguelike community is very welcoming and fun to participate in. There is a lot of incentive to share knowledge and grow together.

Many AAA games are using techniques championed by roguelike development such as procedural generation to improve the replayability of the games and decrease the amount of time used for content creation. Recent indie bestsellers have been relying on procedural generation not only for level design but also for story and enemies. Permadeath adds a layer of difficulty to those games that appeal to a niche but loyal hardcore user base. I can see a trend where more and more mainstays of roguelike development are not only incorporated by major games but are put into the spotlight as reasons why those games are good.

I believe that roguelikes will help you acquire technical skills that are not only directly employable by the general gaming industry but also serve you well in other development. Your creative skills will also improve as you both refine your coding to match your worldbuilding and vice versa.

Storytelling is an important skill to have that will serve you for the rest of your life. The reasons I've quoted so far will help you explain to all your friends and family why you're doing this and justify your investment of time into this craft, but the main reason for developing roguelikes is because you want to develop roguelikes. It is a fun activity and you have an idea, a little gem of mechanics, or theme, or constraint, that you want to explore. There is a little dungeon inside your mind, your ideas are hidden in it, and you want to invite more people in. Yes, you can justify learning roguelike development using many rational arguments regarding career and knowledge, but the best argument is an emotional one: you're doing it because you want to do it.

Why use web technologies?

It is very hard to get someone to actually install some application you've developed, even if it is a wonderful game. Thousands of games appear in the popular application marketplaces every week. It is very hard to get noticed, and studios spend a huge amount of money in marketing just to convince people to give their game a try. The less friction your potential users have in trying out your game, the higher are the chances they will actually do it.

Web technologies allow us to ship games that are playable in a wide range of devices without needing installation. Your web-based game will potentially work on smartphones, tablets, laptops, desktops, and more. You can still prepare those web-based games for distribution in popular gaming marketplaces while still retaining the option to distribute them on your own on the Web. It is the widest reach possible with the least amount of friction. All your users will need to do is open a web page and play the game.

There is another important aspect of using web technologies which is that they can reduce the amount of time between shipping new versions of your game to your users. This is especially important if you're developing a game in the open by constantly updating beta versions while receiving feedback from testers. You won't need to ship new game installers and wait for the testers to update; you'll update a single online web page, and all of them will get and test the latest version. This rapid iteration will prove beneficial not only for the gamers but for you as well as anything that saves you time and headaches will free time and brain space for you to focus on what is really important: your game.

In this book, we'll be focusing mostly on JavaScript and using very little HTML and CSS. JavaScript is a very approachable language which is very forgiving for new developers who are just learning it for the first time and very powerful in the hands of seasoned developers. A novice learner will be able to use it and produce something usable without too many challenges. Not all languages make it easy for new developers to produce something they can show around while they are in the beginner phase and still being useful to actually ship top-of-the-line games in the future. Improving your JavaScript skills through roguelike development is a neat way to level up as a developer.

There are other languages that are faster and provide more control over resource usage than JavaScript. If you want a job in the industry, it will be good to learn them too, but don't think even for a second that JS is not a good investment of your time. As Brendan Eich said, "Always bet on JS!", today's JavaScript engines are very powerful virtual machines which will empower your roguelike designs to the fullest. In this book, you won't find a moment where language and runtime will be a constraint to us. JS will always be an asset and never a limitation in our roguelike journey.

Why Phaser?

There are many wonderful web-based game development frameworks out there. For this book, I've chosen to go with Phaser[4] because it is probably the most popular game development framework available for JavaScript. Working up from Vanilla JavaScript would force us to reimplement lots of low-level game programming patterns. Instead, we are going to use a genre-agnostic general-purpose game development framework. The roguelike part of our code will be implemented by us, but we will be standing on the shoulders of giants and leveraging all the hard work that has been put into that framework for the generic game programming features we'll need.

Phaser is easy to learn and battle tested by thousands of games and gamers. It is a real framework that is used in the industry, and learning it helps you to be closer to what the professionals in the field are using. This framework is used by both hobbyists and professionals alike. It has a lot of learning materials available online for you to study it further, and it is also used by another book from Apress which is focused on multiplayer game development, so by combining these two books, you might end up developing a multiplayer roguelike, right?

Phaser makes it easier to develop games that work across different form factors. This is important to increase the reach of our game as people using both small devices like smartphones and larger devices such as laptops will be able to play our roguelike.

The general lifecycle and workflow of a Phaser game are similar to other frameworks both web based and native. Many of the concepts you'll learn will be transferable if you end up deciding to use something different in the future.

---

[4]https://phaser.io

It is important to notice that Phaser is a general game development framework; it doesn't force or constrain you to some genre or type of game. It is very flexible in that way, and you'll be able to use it in other future projects. That being said, we could be using a library specific for roguelike development, and that would have saved us a huge amount of work by providing ready-made and tested features that are common and important to most roguelikes. I decided against using one of those libraries due to two reasons.

The first and most important is that I think learning Phaser is important for anyone doing web-based games. This makes this book useful beyond roguelikes and also approachable by those who already know Phaser and want to learn more about roguelikes.

The second reason is that by forcing us to reimplement some of those features, we end up getting to understand them in a deeper and more meaningful way than by simply using ready-made packages. This has the positive side effect of making us appreciate more those developers who go through the trouble of making those ready-made roguelike libraries. If you try them out in the future, you'll be better equipped to understand their internal plumbing.

Another important aspect of using Phaser for me is that it allows us to start developing with just a minimal set of tools. We don't need complex boilerplates and tooling just to get started. There are other engines out there that use complex tools, and yes, you could go as complex as you want with your Phaser setup, but I think for this book, that would be too distracting. I want to focus on building a roguelike with Phaser; we'll only add the minimal set of tools we need to get into doing that task. I'll be laser focused on simplicity in this book, but Phaser will serve you on your more complex projects as well.

What we're building

Our project for this book is a small web-based roguelite. We're building just enough features for it to be recognized as a **roguelike** without this book exploding into a thousand-page bible. This project is the initial level of roguelike development; you can go deeper if you like.

One decision I've made regarding the content organization of this book might be controversial so it is better that I explain it now before we start. Most roguelike tutorials start with procedural generation and the dungeons. I'm leaving procedural generation to a later chapter in the book. By the time we reach it, we'll already know how to draw a dungeon and fill it with monsters and treasures and how the gameplay works. This will allow us to play with procedural generation and perceive how it affects gameplay because we'll already have the static gameplay done. It becomes much easier to see how different dungeons, or how stronger more prevalent monsters with smarter behaviors, change the game if those parts of the game are already working. So even if I personally believe that procedural generation is the main cornerstone of roguelikes, I'll only touch this topic in the second half of the book.

First, we'll get to meet the Phaser library and use it to draw a dungeon. Then we're adding a player into it and scripting the game loop. Once that works, we're adding monsters and treasures and multiple levels. Once all those parts are in play, we'll dive into procedural generation.

I hope you're as excited as I am to start coding; in the next chapter, we'll go through the basics of Phaser and play with our first dungeon.

CHAPTER 2

Introduction to Phaser

This is going to be an introductory chapter that focuses on game development concepts and how to use Phaser rather than actually building a roguelike. We'll start slowly by building upon concepts and jargon before we get our coding hands busy and start learning how to build games out of Phaser. After learning these concepts, it will become a lot easier to develop our project for this book.

In this chapter, we're going to go through

- Setting up our tools: Getting our computer ready for development

- Game development concepts: Common jargon and theory needed for developing games

- Phaser states: How to apply those concepts to Phaser

All the other chapters will build upon the foundations constructed in this chapter, but what exactly are we building in this book?

Introducing *Nano Dungeon*

The project for this book is a small roguelite game we're calling *Nano Dungeon.* This game is designed to be simple and serve as an *easy to expand project* for your future roguelike explorations. One important aspect of this game that should be clear in your mind is that we want to

A. A. Garzia, *Roguelike Development with JavaScript,*
https://doi.org/10.1007/978-1-4842-6059-3_2

create a simple archetypical roguelike. We're not aiming for innovative mechanics or gameplay; those will come to you later as you progress on your own personal game development journey. *Nano Dungeon* is more of an exercise to allow us to practice building roguelikes.

Our game will be a fantasy-themed dungeon crawler in which the player will go through multiple procedurally generated levels fighting monsters and acquiring items, until they find a magical item in the deepest level of the dungeon. We'll build this game slowly. We'll begin without using any procedural generation at all and then adding and experimenting with procedural generation later.

The main roguelike characteristics the game will have are

- Procedurally generated content

- Permadeath

- Turn-based action

So, with that in our mind, let us begin with setting up our computer.

Setting up

For *Nano Dungeon*, we're going to use a very simple setup. This is deliberate so that we can focus on the game and not on the infinite amount of choices available for JS developers regarding tooling.

Our main objective with our setup is to have it get out of our way and be invisible while we build the game.

Installing a web server

You'll need to install Node.js[1] to be able to install the web server used in this book. The long-term support version is the one we'll be using; you can find out how to install it from the Node.js homepage at `https://Node.js.org`. Phaser doesn't really require Node.js, and the book samples won't be using it directly. You just need to install a tiny web server so that you are able to run the examples.

Most web-based game projects will use Node.js to build and transpile the game. Transpiling allows the developers to work with the bleeding-edge features of JS while still being able to deploy to most of the browsers out there. Node.js is commonly used to pack the final deliverable version of the game into smaller files for more efficient deployment. In this book, we'll not be doing any of this as the choice of tools to execute these tasks depends not only on each developer's taste but also on the specific requirements of each project.

By using Node.js just as a web server and writing JS that is deployed and executed on the browser exactly as we wrote it, it will be easier to debug and interact with our source code. Another advantage from this approach is that you won't need to learn new tools just to match whatever arbitrary choice I could have made on the stack for this book. The example code in this book is simple and invites experimentation. It's my hope that by having no other tools besides an editor, a browser, and a web server, I'll reduce the friction you'd experience in playing with the code and trying new things. I hope that this simplicity invites you to tinker.

You can verify that Node.js was installed correctly by opening a terminal and executing

```
$ node -v
```

---

[1]Node.js LTS version available from `https://Node.js.org`

It should return the version of the installed Node.js. After making sure Node.js is installed, check if NPM, which is the Node.js Package Manager, is installed as well:

```
$ npm -v
```

You're ready to install a web server now. I've selected a very simple one that has autoreload, which means that once you have your sample open, if you alter any of the files and save, the page will reload automatically. Install it with

```
$ npm i -g live-server
```

That will install the live-server command globally.

Choosing a code editor

Any of the commonly used programming editors should be enough for the project we'll be building, so if you already have a favorite programmer's editor to use with your projects, you're OK to keep using it. If you don't have a preferred choice, I recommend you use either *Visual Studio Code*[2] or *Atom*.[3] Both editors have fantastic support for JS workflows.

Getting the source code

After installing Node.js and your editor of choice, you'll need to grab the *Nano Dungeon* source code. The source code for this book is available on GitHub via the book's product page, located at www.apress.com/ISBN.

---

[2]Visual Studio Code available from https://code.visualstudio.com
[3]Atom available from https://atom.io

There is a top-level folder for each chapter in this book, and in each chapter folder, there are multiple example subfolders for the various samples used in each chapter. Each sample is self-contained and doesn't require files from outside its folder.

Running the examples

On your terminal, go to the folder of the example you want to run. There is a top-level folder for each chapter, and inside each chapter's folder, there are multiple folders containing the various samples used in that chapter.

Execute the command live-server; the server will launch and open a web page with the sample running.

How games work

Before we dive deeper into Phaser and coding, it is good that we understand some common game development concepts. The most important one is what a game loop is. Most games have their gameplay workflow tied to a game loop, and understanding how it works helps you plan and develop all kinds of games.

The game loop is the beating heart of your game; it is what gives it life and animates it. In most games, this heart beats at every frame that is drawn to the screen, so if your game is running at 60 frames per second, then your game loop is running 60 times per second as well.

In each beat of the game loop, it needs to do the same tasks. It needs to figure out what the player is trying to do, then simulate the consequences of those actions, and finally draw that to the screen. Basically, we can summarize a game loop into three stages: acquire player input, simulate world, and draw the result as can be seen in Figure 2-1.

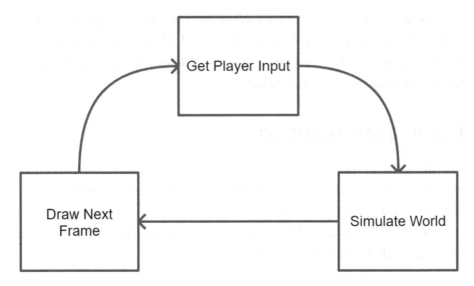

Figure 2-1. *Game loop*

For example, in a (simplified) game of *Pac-Man*, the game loop picks the user input from the arcade joystick and decides in which direction the player is trying to move, and then it calculates the new position for the player. After that, it calculates where each ghost is trying to move and decides on their new position. Finally, it draws the player and the ghosts after they moved a bit. This repeats every frame, giving the illusion of continuous action and movement.

The game loop for a (simplified) *Tetris* game is easy to infer as well. Find out which direction the player is trying to move the falling piece, compute the new position of the piece, and collide this piece with the other pieces, removing the necessary parts of them if they form a line. Check if the accumulated jumble of pieces has reached the top, in which case is game over.

In action games, the game loop usually runs as often as it can and tends to match the *frames per second* value. In turn-based games, it used to be common for the game loop to block waiting for player input and only run a single interaction before blocking again waiting for future input.

These days, even turn-based games are running game loops at the same frequency as their frames per second rate and emulating the turn-based mechanics on top of it. This simplifies animation and other parts of the game and is usually a consequence of using ready-made game genre-agnostic libraries such as Phaser which doesn't offer any special turn-based game feature in its core.

In *Nano Dungeon*, we'll run the game loop as often as we can, but we'll only cause changes to the world if there has been an input from the player. This way, the rest of the game world doesn't act while the player is pondering about their next move.

It is now time to learn how this concept applies to Phaser-based games.

Introducing Phaser

We'll use *Phaser 3*[4] for *Nano Dungeon*. There is a lot of material online about Phaser, and it is very easy to find material regarding Phaser 2 instead of 3 when searching the Web. Be aware that even though both libraries are called Phaser, the API of Phaser 2 and 3 are not the same. You won't be able to use Phaser 2 code with our project.

Phaser is a very flexible framework, and you can use it to build simple toys or complex fully featured games. This means that there are a lot of features from Phaser that we'll not be using in this book as they are not applicable to our simple game. The documentation[5] for Phaser is very comprehensive; don't hesitate to check it out if you want to learn more about any of the APIs shown in this book.

The first concept we need to understand to start coding is Phaser scenes.

---

[4]Phaser 3 available from `https://phaser.io`
[5]Phaser documentation: `https://photonstorm.github.io/phaser3-docs/`

Phaser scenes

A Phaser game is organized in scenes. Each scene contains its own game loop, and some games are simple enough to be composed of a single scene. You can think of scenes as the states your game goes through. A typical arcade game could have a scene for the title screen, another for the options screen, a scene for gameplay, and two scenes for the end of the game, one for winning and another for losing. As the player plays the games, it flows through these scenes organically as needed. Most of our examples will be a single scene.

Let's create the most simple scene and work through the code line by line together. The code for this sample is inside the `chapter-2/example-1-simple-scene/` folder.

A simple scene

Our sample for this section contains an HTML file, a JS file, and some auxiliary assets to load a bitmap font. The HTML used is quite simple; its only function is to load the JS file.

chapter-2/example-1/index.html

```
<!DOCTYPE html>
<head>
    <title>Chapter 2 - Example 1 - Simple Scene</title>
    <script src="phaser.js"></script>
</head>

<body>
    <div id="game"></div>
    <script src="game.js"></script>
</body>

</html>
```

The focus for this sample will be on the JS file which will insert our Phaser scene in the div#game contained in that HTML. I'll show the JS source here and explain it afterward.

chapter-2/example-1/game.js

```
const scene = {
    preload: function () {
        this.load.bitmapFont("arcade", "font/arcade.png", ↵
        "font/arcade.xml");
    },
    create: function (){
        this.add.bitmapText(400, 300, "arcade", ↵
        "Hello Phaser").setOrigin(0.5);
    }
}

const config = {
    type: Phaser.AUTO,
    width: 800,
    height: 600,
    backgroundColor: "#000",
    parent: "game",
    pixelArt: true,
    scene: scene,
    physics: {
        default: "arcade",
        arcade: {
            gravity: { y: 0 }
        }
    }
};

const game = new Phaser.Game(config);
```

21

The game configuration object

To start a game in Phaser, there must be a configuration object describing what are the parameters used to initialize the library. These parameters are defined in the `config` object in our sample. There are some self-explanatory properties such as `width`, `height`, and `backgroundColor` that are easy to understand. Others require further explanation.

The `type` property tells Phaser which renderer to use. There are two possible renderers; it's either a canvas-based renderer or a WebGL-based renderer. The WebGL is better, but it is not supported in all browser and device combinations. Using `Phaser.AUTO` lets Phaser choose the best option for the device it is running.

The `parent` property is used to point to which HTML element should be used to hold the game. In our case, we're pointing it to whatever element has an `id` of game, which for our HTML is a `<div>`.

Usually, Phaser will use some smoothing and antialiasing routines in the graphics you draw to the screen; we're disabling these by setting the `pixelArt` property to `true` which will make our roguelike feel more old-school and pretty.

The `physics` property is a bit more complex. Phaser has different physics engines bundled with it that are able to simulate how things should behave in the real world. These engines vary in their complexity and features so you are able to choose what is the best option for your game. They are not the kind of engine used for scientific simulations; what they provide is a set of features and mechanics that help you implement your game world physics system in terms of gravity, speeding bullets, collisions, and so on. This is especially useful for arcade games which make use of moving and shooting entities. We're not using this in this sample, but it felt best to explain it anyway because we have to add it to the game configuration object. What that property is doing in the sample is selecting the arcade engine which is the most simple physics engine bundled with Phaser and setting the gravity on the y axis to zero because we're making a top view game, and we don't want things falling south of the game screen as if that was the bottom of the world.

The last entry in our game configuration points at the scene to be loaded which is the topic for the next section.

The scene object

That sample uses a very simple scene object compared to the future samples used in this book; nevertheless, it is a good opportunity for us to begin to understand more about such object as they will be the most used Phaser concept throughout the whole book.

A Phaser scene can be built using either an object or a class; in this sample, we're using an object. The lifecycle of a scene passes through different states, and the developer is free to implement only the states that make sense for their scene. These states are JS functions that are called in a synchronous flow so that each callback is only invoked after the previous one completes as can be seen in Figure 2-2.

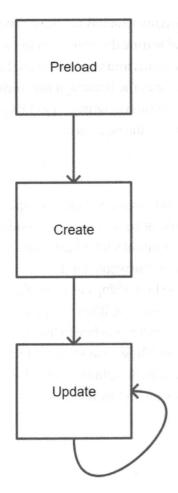

Figure 2-2. *Scene lifecycle*

Phaser first calls the preload function which gives you the opportunity to preload any external asset you need. In our sample, we're loading a bitmap font. These fonts use an image and an XML file, so we pass them both in the code:

```
this.load.bitmapFont("arcade", "font/arcade.png", "font/ ↵
arcade.xml");
```

There is a loader plugin in Phaser which you normally interact using `this.load.*`; in our case, we're using the loader for `bitmapFonts` and naming our font `arcade`. This name will be used in a later lifecycle callback.

After `preload`, Phaser will call `create`; this callback function is used to set up your scene for display for the first time. Our code for this sample just adds a text to the center of the screen.

```
this.add.bitmapText(400, 300, "arcade", "Hello Phaser") ↵
.setOrigin(0.5);
```

Similarly to the loaded plugin, there is another scene plugin which is a `GameObjectFactory`. This is a fancy name that makes it sound more complicated to understand than it actually is. What it does is facilitate adding game objects to a scene; you'll usually interact with it using `this.add.*`. In our sample, we're adding a `bitmapText` at the 400x300 coordinates to write *Hello Phaser* using the `arcade` font. An important concept we should talk more about before moving to the final section of the code is coordinate systems and what that `.setOrigin(0.5)` is doing at the end of the `create` code.

Phaser is primarily a 2D game engine in which we draw things using a two-axis system. The coordinates start on 0x0 which is the top-left corner of the canvas and grows both downward and rightward. This might be counterintuitive for the mathematically inclined among us, but it is how most of the computer graphic engines work.

When we add a game object to the screen using `this.add.*`, the coordinate we pass is anchored on the top-left corner of our game object. This means that if we pass the coordinates for the middle of the screen, the game object we're adding will end up with its top-left corner in that coordinate and its body a bit below that and to the right.

The best way to position something that we want centered is by altering how these coordinates are anchored in a given game object by changing its origin. You can reposition the coordinate that is considered the origin for any game object using setOrigin on them. You can learn more about that routine by reading its documentation;[6] here we're passing a single argument to it, 0.5, which causes the origin to be repositioned halfway on the x and the y axis for that game object. In summary, setOrigin(0.5) causes the origin coordinate for an object to change from the top-left corner to the center of the object, making it a lot easier to place it onto the screen in the position we want.

The final line of the code initializes the game object and causes the sample to load

```
const game = new Phaser.Game(config);
```

To see the sample, you need to load the HTML with a web server. If you followed the steps outlined in the beginning of this chapter and installed live-server, you can use your terminal to go into chapter-2/example-1-simple-scene/ folder and execute live-server. The server will start and your browser will open. You should see the sample running like this:

Chapter 2, Example 1: Running in a web browser

---

[6]setOrigin documentation: https://photonstorm.github.io/phaser3-docs/ Phaser.GameObjects.Components.Origin.html#setOrigin

26

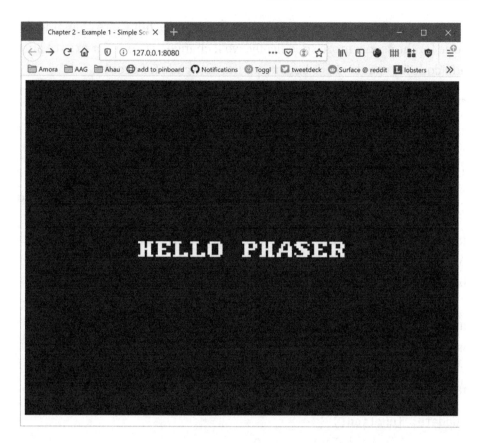

This sample doesn't contain all the lifecycle methods displayed on Figure 2-2; it only sports the first two callbacks: `preload` and `create`; there is no `update` in it which means that scene is a static scene that once created never changes.

Instead of adding more code to this sample, let's switch to the second sample for this chapter. Please open the content for the `chapter-2/example-2-scene-with-update/` folder in your favorite editor. The content for this new sample is the same as the previous one, but we're changing the code for the scene; more specifically, we'll change the code for create and add code for update. Let's begin with the new code for create:

```
create: function () {
  this.helloText = this.add.bitmapText(400, 300, "arcade", ↵
  "Hello Phaser").setOrigin(0.5);
}
```

The change in this code is that instead of just adding the bitmapText to the screen center, we're assigning the resulting value from that operation to the this.helloText property. Since both create and update will belong to the same object, we can use this.* to pass game objects around between the lifecycle functions.

As seen in Figure 2-2, the update function calls itself over and over and is the beating heart of your game loop. Our objective for this sample is to make our "Hello Phaser" text move toward the right of the screen vanishing and then reappearing from the left side much like those ticker tape screens you see in movies.

```
update: function() {
        this.helloText.x += 10

        if (this.helloText.x > 1000) {
            this.helloText.x = -200
        }
    }
```

We can access the bitmapText added to the scene in create by using this this.helloText reference. Game objects have lots of useful methods and properties, which we'll explain more as the book progresses, but for this sample, we're only interested in the x coordinate for the object. In each update cycle, we're incrementing the object position in the x axis by 10 pixels. If we don't do anything else, the text will vanish to the right, never to come back. To avoid that and give that ticker tape effect, there is an if clause check to see if the text is offscreen (remember that the canvas is only 800 pixels wide, so if the text x position is 1000, the text is beyond the right side of the canvas) and reposition it before the left side of the screen by using a negative x coordinate.

Loading that demo by using the live-server web server on that folder will launch the sample, and you'll be able to see the ticker tape effect.

This sample contains all the lifecycle methods that we're going to use for most of the *Nano Dungeon* game implementation. Still, if we reason about it using the processes outlined in Figure 2-1, you'll notice that we're just doing two of the three steps shown there: we're *simulating the world* and then *drawing the next frame*; there is no user input in this sample or the sample before it. Before this chapter ends, we need to add that so we have a full interactive game loop.

Open chapter-2/example-3-interactive-gameloop/ in your editor. Again there are changes to both create and update.

In create, we're adding a property to the object to allow us to check the state of the cursor keys from the update function. Our objective is to allow the user to move the text around using the cursor keys. To do that, we'll use the createCursorKeys()[7] function from the keyboard plugin, a handy function that returns an object that will reflect the state of the four arrow keys from the computer keyboard:

```
create: function () {
  this.helloText = this.add.bitmapText(400, 300, "arcade", ↵
  "Hello Phaser").setOrigin(0.5);
  this.cursors = this.input.keyboard.createCursorKeys();
}
```

[7]createCursorKeys() documentation: https://photonstorm.github.io/phaser3-docs/Phaser.Input.Keyboard.KeyboardPlugin.html#createCursorKeys__anchor

In update, we're going to check each of the cursor keys in a sequence and change the position of the text according to which key is pressed:

```
update: function () {
    if (this.cursors.left.isDown) {
        this.helloText.x -= 10;
    }

    if (this.cursors.right.isDown) {
        this.helloText.x += 10;
    }

    if (this.cursors.up.isDown) {
        this.helloText.y -= 10;

    }

    if (this.cursors.down.isDown) {
        this.helloText.y += 10;
    }
}
```

For each key pressed, we add or subtract 10 pixels from the position of the text to move it in the direction being pressed. Launch that demo and you'll be able to control the position of the text using the arrow keys on your computer keyboard.

Exercise

Can you mix the ticker tape sample and the interactive game loop so that if the player moves the text offscreen, it reappears from the other side?

Summary

We covered a lot of ground in this chapter. The key takeaways that you need to make sure you're comfortable with before we move on are

- The concept of game loops and how they are the beating heart of the game

- The lifecycle of a Phaser scene with `preload`, `create`, and `update`

On our next chapter, we'll start coding a roguelike, and by the end of it, instead of a simple "Hello Phaser" in the screen, we'll have a dungeon and a player character.

CHAPTER 3

Dungeoning

In the previous chapter, we learned how to draw things to the screen and how to create a basic game loop. This chapter will build on that foundation to assemble a basic dungeon for our roguelike, but before delving into some more coding, it is important to understand a bit more about tilemaps and how they are used to assemble a dungeon.

What are tilemaps?

Tilemaps were initially used to save space and memory in games running in older computers and video game consoles. Instead of having a gigantic image with the whole level for a game, the level graphics could be assembled by combining smaller chunks together. This way, the game could only get and draw the chunks needed to display whatever the player was seeing at the moment instead of loading a potentially much larger file into memory. This had the side effect of making much easier to create level editors as the components used by a game level were separate and easy to place in new level designs. They also proved to be a good match for procedural generation as a program could create an algorithmically generated level and then find which tiles it needed to assemble it for display.

For our purposes, we define tilemaps as a grid where we place square-shaped bitmaps in each cell to assemble a dungeon and the necessary game elements. If you ever played a pen and paper role-playing

© Andre Alves Garzia 2020
A. A. Garzia, *Roguelike Development with JavaScript*,
https://doi.org/10.1007/978-1-4842-6059-3_3

game like *Dungeons & Dragons*, and had to draw a map using graph paper, you'll notice a lot of similarities between that and what our software for this chapter will do.

The dungeon used for the book's roguelike project will eventually have multiple levels. Each level will be a tilemapped grid where walls, rooms, corridors, and other elements are placed to assemble a recognizable RPG-like dungeon. Let's learn how to draw some tiles.

Drawing a tilemap

The source code for this section is under the `chapter-3/example-1-simple-tilemap` folder; you'll need it to follow along. The HTML file is the same as the other samples; it just loads Phaser and our `game.js` file which is where all the interesting bits for this section are actually happening.

Preloading a spritesheet

A spritesheet is an image file that combines many different graphics into a single file. Web games tend to use them because they require a single network transfer to land all the necessary images into the player's computer.

The kind of spritesheet our sample uses is a simple one where all images have the same size and they are placed side by side much like a very well-organized collection of stamps on a page. For example, suppose each image is 10 pixels by 10 pixels and you have ten images in two rows in the spritesheet, that means you have a single image file that is 20 pixels tall by 50 pixels wide with all your images inside.

People often call these images contained in a spritesheet sprite, but you'll also see the same noun being applied to game elements which are moving on the screen, which might be confusing if you're new to game development and are searching online for learning material. I'm going to call them tiles unless they refer to game elements that represent stuff that moves such as the player or monsters. They are all coming from the same file though.

Our spritesheet is from a freely available game art pack by Kenney,[1] and it looks gorgeous (Figure 3-1).

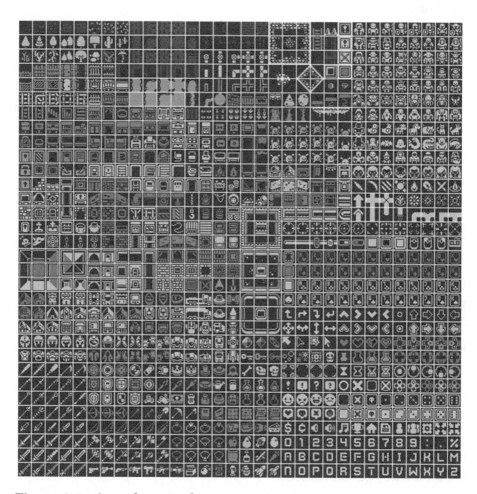

Figure 3-1. *Sample spritesheet*

---

[1]Kenney 1-bit art pack: www.kenney.nl/assets/bit-pack

As can be seen, there are many different tiles in it, and we'll be able to combine them for a rich roguelike experience. Each image in this spritesheet is a square with 16 pixels on each side. They are separated by gaps of 1 pixel. The source code for preloading the spritesheet needs all this information to be passed. From the game.js file, the preload() function is

```
preload: function () {
    this.load.spritesheet(
        'tiles',
        'assets/colored.png',
        {
            frameWidth: 16,
            frameHeight: 16,
            spacing: 1
        });
}
```

Much like other preload() functions we've seen, we use a function in the this.load.* namespace to load the spritesheet. The arguments for that function are the key we'll use to refer to that spritesheet later, the path to the spritesheet image, and a configuration object. There are many optional parameters that can be set in this configuration object; we're just setting the dimensions of each image in the sheet and the gap between them.

With that in place, we're ready to start drawing some tilemaps, which are grids like graph paper you might have used in school, in which we place tiles in each cell to form our dungeon image. The tiles will come from the spritesheet we saw earlier.

A basic tilemap

To represent the tilemap grid, we'll use a bidimensional array where each element is a number that matches a tile in our spritesheet. A 5x5 dungeon with textured floor on each side and empty floor everywhere else would be represented as

```
let dungeon = [
    [1,1,1,1,1],
    [1,0,0,0,1],
    [1,0,0,0,1],
    [1,0,0,0,1],
    [1,1,1,1,1]
]
```

And this would lead to a dungeon that looks like:

If you check the spritesheet, you'll see that the floor areas are the first image in the sheet and that textured floor on each side is the second image. Since arrays in JavaScript are zero indexed, those become *image 0* and *image 1* from the spritesheet.

There is an important caveat in building the map array. If you use numbers matching the spritesheet indexes and later you change the spritesheet, you'll end up needing to change all the maps or creating some routine to remap those numbers at runtime. It is better to craft a map with numbers that make sense for you and your design and remap those numbers to values that correspond to the desired tiles in the spritesheet just before drawing the map to the screen. This way, if you ever change the spritesheet you're using, you'll only need to change that mapping data.

The create() function is where we'll assemble our tilemap. The map used in the sample code for this section uses a 10x10 map.

```
let level = [
    [1, 1, 1, 1, 1, 1, 1, 1, 1, 1],
    [1, 0, 0, 0, 0, 0, 0, 0, 0, 1],
    [1, 0, 0, 0, 0, 0, 0, 0, 0, 1],
    [1, 0, 0, 0, 0, 0, 0, 0, 0, 1],
    [1, 0, 0, 0, 0, 0, 0, 0, 0, 1],
    [1, 0, 0, 0, 0, 0, 0, 0, 0, 1],
    [1, 0, 0, 0, 0, 0, 0, 0, 0, 1],
    [1, 0, 0, 0, 0, 0, 0, 0, 0, 1],
    [1, 0, 0, 0, 0, 0, 0, 0, 0, 1],
    [1, 1, 1, 1, 1, 1, 1, 1, 1, 1],
]
```

We're mapping 0 to mean floor and 1 to mean wall in our map. After it, we need to remap them to the correct values for the tilemap we're using. The floor in the spritesheet is indeed the same value as the value we're using, but for the wall, we're going to use image 554 which is a brick wall.

```
const wall = 554
const floor = 0
level = level.map(r => r.map(t => t == 1 ? wall : floor))
```

To draw that tilemap to the screen, we need to create a configuration object holding the information about it to hold the level data and the dimensions for each tile. Since our tiles are 16 pixels square, we store that value in a constant because we are going to use it multiple times during this sample.

```
const tileSize = 16
const config = {
    data: level,
    tileWidth:  tileSize,
    tileHeight: tileSize,
}
```

Let's use that configuration object to create a tilemap and attach a tileset to it. The tileset is what will match our spritesheet to the tilemap.

```
const map = this.make.tilemap(config);
const tileset = map.addTilesetImage('tiles', 'tiles', ↵
tileSize, tileSize, 0, 1);
```

A tilemap is created by passing the configuration object to this. make.tilemap(), and then an inherited function attached to the new map is used to add the tileset image to it. You can create all sorts of game objects using functions from this.make.*; they are part of the GameObjectCreator class.[2]

That addTilesetImage[3] function is receiving a lot of arguments; most of them are optional, but I've noticed that if I don't pass them in this sample, the map doesn't work.

[2]GameObjectCreator class documentation: https://photonstorm.github.io/ phaser3-docs/Phaser.GameObjects.GameObjectCreator.html
[3]Documentation for addTilesetImage: https://photonstorm.github.io/ phaser3-docs/Phaser.Tilemaps.Tilemap.html#addTilesetImage__anchor

Phaser supports many different map data formats beyond the arrays we're using. Many developers use map editors such as Tiled[4] to build their maps. These editors can export the map in rich formats which Phaser can import. Since we're not using such tools, we end up having to specify a lot of data that would be present in the exported map data by hand.

The first argument to `addTilesetImage` is the tileset name as exported in the map data. We don't have a map data as we're not using a map editor. We're passing `tiles` which is the same key we used in the spritesheet loading. The second argument is the key of the cached image from `preload()`, which is `tiles`. If we don't pass this second parameter, it uses the first one as the key to look for the image; it is a bit confusing. We just pass them both to be clear about what we're doing. The rest of the arguments are all data that would be present in the export from a map editor, all of which we need to explicitly pass since we're assembling everything by hand. The third and fourth arguments are the tile dimensions, their width and height. The fifth and sixth arguments are related to the margin around the spritesheet and the gap between images. All values are in pixels.

Phaser's tilemaps can have multiple layers in them, much like placing acetate sheets on top of each other in classic old-school animation or working with Adobe Photoshop layers. The layers can be used to separate game elements into background and foreground layers so that they can appear on top of each other.

There are two types of layers, dynamic and static; the former trades some speed and performance to be able to apply powerful per tile effects. For the tilemap we'll be drawing in this sample, we're going to use a static tilemap since we're not doing any kind of such effects at the moment.

```
const ground = map.createStaticLayer(0, tileset, 0, 0);
```

---

[4]Tiled map editor: `www.mapeditor.org/`

Even though we're assigning our static layer to the ground variable, we're not doing anything with it later. It is just to document that that is the ground layer, where the floor and walls are. The first argument to `createStaticLayer()` is the layer ID; this can be either a number or a string and is used by other functions to refer to the layer. We're using 0 because naming it with a string is used only when you're loading maps exported from the Tiled map editor. The second argument is the tileset you created previously.

If you load that sample in your browser, you'll see a tilemap that looks like Figure 3-2.

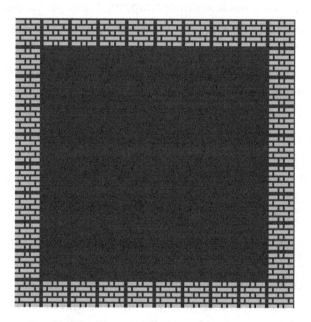

Figure 3-2. Basic tilemap

And that is how you draw a tilemap. There was a lot to digest in this section, and it is very beneficial to check the linked documentation for the Phaser functions. Another important exercise to do now is experiment with that map array and different values. Can you place four pillars in that room? A skeleton on the ground?

What about drawing a dungeon? Well, that is our next sample.

A basic dungeon

It is important at this point to understand why I left the procedural generation part of the book to future chapters. Many people think that the foremost feature of a roguelike is procedural generation; to be honest, I'm on that camp as well.

Still, if we leave it to later chapters in the book, we can nail down lots of the basic mechanics of our game and have a better understanding of Phaser and game development by the time we reach those chapters. This way, we can play with procedural generation and appreciate how it alters and enriches the whole game development experience instead of learning both game development basics and procedural generation at the same time.

The next sample is in the `chapter-3/example-2-basic-dungeon` folder, and it is exactly the same code as the previous sample. The only change is that we alter the level array to be a real dungeon-like map instead of a 10 by 10 simple grid. Another small change was to alter the `game.js` included in the HTML to mark it as a *JavaScript module* so that we can use `import` inside it to load the map data from a different file. The level data has been placed outside the main source code because it is massive, which is also the reason why I'm not pasting it in here.

Load it and you'll see a dungeon like Figure 3-3.

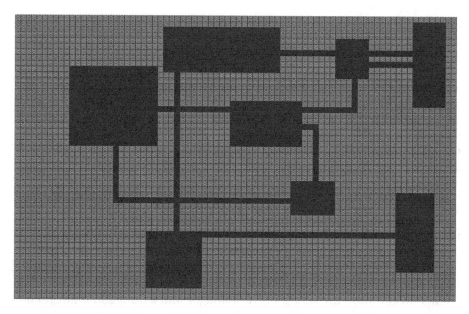

Figure 3-3. *Basic dungeon*

Adding a player character

This sample will be quite familiar as it combines techniques we learned in this and the previous chapters. The folder for it is chapter-3/example-3-playable-dungeon. As our sample code grows and reuses parts of the previous samples, I'll only show what changed or what is new. It is best to read these chapters with the source code open in your computer or at least refer to that code later before moving on to the next chapters.

Our player character image is coming from the same spritesheet as the dungeon elements, so we don't need to change the sample preload() function to load any extra image file.

In Chapter 2, we built a simple game loop that allowed us to change the position of the displayed text by reading the state of the arrow keys in the update() function. A similar approach would suit an action RPG more than the roguelike we're building because those games tend to rely more on quick real-time action than the tactical pondering that turn-based games are usually known for. Phaser is genre agnostic, but it is a bit biased toward real-time action and has many built-in features that support such use case. Being turn based is one of the requirements we placed on our roguelike which means that we need to build our own turn-based mechanics on top of what Phaser offers.

This is the point in our source code where things start becoming more complex in terms of organization and planning. Adding a player character may sound like a simple task, but to accomplish that, we are going to have to implement lots of features that are a part of the core game mechanics. It is a lot of work, but by breaking it down into smaller pieces, we'll be able to handle it. A key step in making all this manageable is to stop throwing everything inside `preload()`, `create()`, and `update()` and start building little modules and classes to help. In this sample, we're going to build some new modules including a turn manager and a dungeon manager and a player character class.

Much of the abstractions and workflows present in this book are coming from pen and paper RPGs and wargames. If you've never played one of those, I think it is beneficial to learn more about them as you read this book. There are many YouTube channels and podcasts that record play sessions, including play sessions with professional actors. Spending some time checking those games out might flesh out the mechanics we're building here in this chapter.

It begins with a dungeon manager

As mentioned earlier, Phaser has a ton of features, but it is not biased toward roguelikes. To create a more ergonomic project, we're going to build auxiliary modules that abstract some of Phaser away so that we can think more in terms of our roguelike than in terms of Phaser.

The main responsibility of our dungeon manager is to load the level and connect the Phaser plumbing necessary to show it on the screen. Some of the code that was in the `create()` function in the previous sample will now be a part of the dungeon module. As our roguelike becomes more complex, this module will accrue more and more functionality. For this sample, we'll use it to load our premade level and create the necessary tilemap, tileset, and dynamic layer for our game. We need to switch to a dynamic layer because the player will be moving on that layer, and in a static layer, it is impossible to change tiles.

In the future, when we start doing procedural generation, this module internals can be changed while the rest of the game remains the same. Part of the refactoring of these routines into it is preparing the groundwork for those future chapters.

These are the responsibilities of the dungeon manager:

- Loading the premade level

- Remapping the numbers used in that level to tiles from our spritesheet

- Creating the tileset, tilemap, and dynamic layer used by our map

The code for the dungeon manager is inside the *dungeon.js*; let's go over it. We're using ES6 modules; if their usage and structure are not clear to you, check out the documentation about them at MDN Web Docs.[5]

We begin by importing the level data:

```
import level from "./level.js"
```

---

[5]JavaScript modules documentation: https://developer.mozilla.org/en-US/docs/Web/JavaScript/Guide/Modules

All of the code for the dungeon manager is contained in an object literal called dungeon which we export as the *default export* at the end of the file. Inside the dungeon object, we create a sprites literal object to map human-readable keys to the values used by our spritesheet.

```
sprites: {
    floor: 0,
    wall: 554,
}
```

We'll use those values later in a mapping function much like the chapter-3/example-1-simple-tilemap/ sample did.

An initialize() function is used to handle all the code that was previously handled by the create() inside our previous samples. This function receives the current scene that is calling it as an argument.

```
initialize: function (scene) {
    this.scene = scene

    scene.level = level.map(r => r.map(t => t == 1 ? ⏎
    this.sprites.wall : this.sprites.floor))

    const tileSize = 16
    const config = {
        data: scene.level,
        tileWidth: tileSize,
        tileHeight: tileSize,
    }

    const map = scene.make.tilemap(config)
    const tileset = map.addTilesetImage('tiles', 'tiles', 16, ⏎
    16, 0, 1)
    this.map = map.createDynamicLayer(0, tileset, 0, 0)
}
```

It first saves a reference to the scene because in the future our game entities will import the dungeon manager and might need to do something to the scene.

As can be seen, the code is a combination of the first and second samples for this chapter as it uses a mapping call to replace the ones in the map with the corresponding wall value from the spritesheet like the first sample, but it is using an externally loaded level data like the second sample.

The rest of the code is almost a copy and paste from the previous one but with some important changes. The dynamic layer created is saved to dungeon.map; this will be used by the player character class to inspect the map and decide upon its movement. Before we implement the player class, we must talk about turns and turn management.

Creating a turn manager

There are many ways to code a turn manager. Game developers can overengineer this as much as they want, and part of the charm of a roguelike can actually be the nifty complex ways the turn mechanics play out.

My favorite turn-based computer games all had the same mechanics regarding turn management: each character would have an amount of points to use in their turn, doing actions would cost points, and the turn was over when you were out of points. Phaser will call update many times per second so we can't simply block the actions there and handle player input in an imperative way. We'll have to code our own turn manager on top of the frequent calls to update to implement the mechanics I outlined at the start of the paragraph. The code will resemble a state machine; each game entity will change their state between having points to spend, being out of points, and refreshing their points. A simple way of implementing a turn manager is simply handling the player movement as in an action game and, after each move, iterating over the other game entities and their actions. Our sample will do something a bit more involved than that without actually going toward a super complex solution; our objective will be to implement mechanics that are similar to the ones outlined earlier.

All our game entities, may they be the player, monsters, or something else we invent in the future, will be new JS classes. These classes will necessarily implement the following methods:

Method	Explanation
turn()	Called when it is their turn. Should perform all actions needed for that turn.
over()	Returns a Boolean flagging if the turn for that entity is over or not.
refresh()	Called before a new turn takes place.

At the beginning of a turn, our manager will call refresh() on each entity. Then each entity will perform their turn(). If over() returns true for all entities, a new turn begins. The reason behind having an over() method is so that if you don't return true in it, that entity will get another call to turn(). This enables an entity to have many actions per turn in the future, such as creating a monster that moves many tiles in a turn while the player moves just one. This can instill fear in the player quite easily.

The turn manager is in its own module inside turnManager.js; it is a singleton and is used by the update() code in game.js. The code is inside a literal object called tm (short for turn manager, makes it easier to paste code in the book because it is shorter). We'll use a JavaScript Set[6] to hold

---

[6]MDN Web Docs documentation for Sets: https://developer.mozilla.org/en-US/docs/Web/JavaScript/Reference/Global_Objects/Set

the entities present in the dungeon and provide functions to add and remove entities from this set besides that it mimics the preceding workflow by having turn(), over(), and refresh() functions that call the similarly named functions for each entity present in the set.

Let's go over the code used for managing entities.

```
entities: new Set(),
addEntity: (entity) => tm.entities.add(entity),
removeEntity: (entity) => tm.entities.remove(entity),
```

Using a Set() to hold an entity prevents us from adding the same entity twice; these kinds of bugs are sometimes hard to track down so using a data structure that doesn't support adding the same entity more than once makes our code safer. There are two functions, one for adding an entity and another for removing it; we're not using the remove function in this sample, but we'll use it in the future so it was easier to implement it already.

Next, let's implement the code for turn() which is responsible for calling the turn() method of each entity. As written earlier, we could've opted for a simpler turn manager, but I don't think it would be as fun as this one. What the turn() function does is to loop over the entities set, checking if each entity turn is over(); if it is not, then it picks that entity and calls its turn() method and then *breaks the loop*.

This breaking is important because it enables the turn() for that entity to be called again before calling turn() on other entities as the loop will run again from the start after the break during the next scene update() call, thus allowing our entities to have *multiple actions per turn* which will come in handy once we start building new character classes and monsters.

Phaser runs the scene update() cycle very fast; that's how the game gets 60 fps. The problem with that is that if we simply call tm.turn() on each update(), our game runs too fast. What I mean by that is that if our player presses the down arrow key to move its character down a tile and we're running at 60 fps, then the key will register as pressed down for multiple iterations of the update() cycle, causing the character to sprint in that direction very fast. Our turn handling mechanics are not broken, they'd just be running new turns very fast.

To cope with that, there is a simple debouncing code in the turn manager. It keeps track of when turn() last run in milliseconds and only allows it to be called again if 150 milliseconds passed since the last call. It is like putting a break on a fast car so that you can move a bit slower and enjoy the view. We store a property in the tm object called lastCall and initialize it with the current date; there is also an interval property that is set to the amount of milliseconds we want to wait between turns.

```
turn: () => {
    let now = Date.now()
    let limit = tm.lastCall + tm.interval
    if (now > limit) {
        for (let e of tm.entities) {
            if (!e.over()) {
                e.turn()
                break;
            }
        }
        tm.lastCall = Date.now()
    }
}
```

The most interesting part is the breakable loop as mentioned earlier. With that module done, it becomes much easier to implement and understand the player class.

The player class

The player character is a class not because we're thinking about implementing multiple players, but because this will be the pattern used by other game entities, and once we implement other character types, they can inherit from this base class. The code for the player class is inside player.js.

The player class, which is the default export of player.js, imports the dungeon manager which is a singleton so it has access to the scene and the level data to calculate its movement.

In this game entity, we're using the concept of movement points which is common in wargames and tactical RPG games. Basically, a game entity has a quantity of movement points to use per turn. Each time they move, they spend a movement point. Once the movement points of the entity reach zero, their turn() is over(). Our player character will start with one movement point and in each refresh() will get that point back. In the future, once we add more complexity to the game, we'll have other points as well, but for now that is all we need since this sample is only concerned with movement.

The constructor for our player class receives as argument the coordinates where the player character is placed on the map. In that function, we store the coordinates, create and store the cursor keys used for movement, store a reference to the sprite used for that character, and draw it in the map (which the class has access because it imported the dungeon module).

```
constructor(x, y) {
    this.movementPoints = 1
    this.cursors = dungeon.scene.input.keyboard.createCursorKeys()
    this.x = x
    this.y = y
    this.sprite = 29

    dungeon.map.putTileAt(this.sprite, this.x, this.y)
}
```

Besides storing a bunch of references for future use, there is a function which we haven't seen before: putTileAt().[7] This is from the dynamic layer class and allows us to place a different tile at a given coordinate. We'll use that to simulate the player movement in the map by switching the destination tile sprite with the player character sprite and the previous location back to the floor sprite.

Implementing both refresh() and over() is easy now that we understand the mechanics.

```
refresh() {
    this.movementPoints = 1
}
over() {
    return this.movementPoints == 0
}
```

Quite straightforward isn't it? The turn() function is a bit more involved, and it resembles the code used in Chapter 2 to move the text. At the beginning of the turn() function, we store the current player's position and create a Boolean to store if the player moved or not.

```
let oldX = this.x
let oldY = this.y
let moved = false
```

[7]Phaser 3 documentation for putTileAt: https://photonstorm.
github.io/phaser3-docs/Phaser.Tilemaps.DynamicTilemapLayer.
html#putTileAt__anchor

Then, check if the player has movement points left; check each cursor key and update coordinates as needed.

```
if (this.movementPoints > 0) {
    if (this.cursors.left.isDown) {
        this.x -= 1
        moved = true
    }

    if (this.cursors.right.isDown) {
        this.x += 1
        moved = true
    }

    if (this.cursors.up.isDown) {
        this.y -= 1
        moved = true
    }

    if (this.cursors.down.isDown) {
        this.y += 1
        moved = true
    }

    if (moved) {
        this.movementPoints -= 1
    }
}
```

If moved is true, subtract a point from the movement points. This is what will eventually cause over() to return true and end the player's turn. By the end of that part of the code, the coordinates for the player character will be at the new position, but the screen is not updated yet, so we can actually revert the movement if the player is actually moving into a wall.

```
let tileAtDestination = dungeon.map.getTileAt(this.x, this.y)
if (tileAtDestination.index == dungeon.sprites.wall) {
    this.x = oldX
    this.y = oldY
}
```

The getTileAt()[8] function is the inverse function of putTileAt() which we've seen before. Finally, it is just a matter of drawing the player character in the new position and flipping the tile in the old position to a floor tile.

```
if (this.x !== oldX || this.y !== oldY) {
    dungeon.map.putTileAt(this.sprite, this.x, this.y)
    dungeon.map.putTileAt(dungeon.sprites.floor, oldX, oldY)
}
```

The player class is now complete. It doesn't do much except handling movement, but that is our current project. It is time to integrate all of this back into the scene.

---

[8]Phaser 3 documentation for getTileAt(): https://photonstorm.github.io/
phaser3-docs/Phaser.Tilemaps.DynamicTilemapLayer.html#getTileAt__anchor

Updating the scene

The game.js file for this sample is much simpler than the previous ones since we extracted most of the logic contained in them into the modules we just implemented. It is quite similar to the previous sample, but at the top, we start by importing our new modules and the player class.

```
import dungeon from "./dungeon.js"
import tm from "./turnManager.js"
import PlayerCharacter from "./player.js"
```

Compared to the previous sample, the only changes are to the create() and update() functions. The preload() remains the same and just loads the spritesheet.

Look at how streamlined the new create() function is:

```
create: function () {
    dungeon.initialize(this)
    let player = new PlayerCharacter(15, 15)
    tm.addEntity(player)
}
```

It just initializes the dungeon manager passing the scene itself, and then it creates a new player instance and adds it to the turn manager.

The update() function is also quite simple. It checks to see if the turns are over(); if they are, then all entities are refresh() and then turn() is called over and over again.

```
update: function () {
    if (tm.over()) {
        tm.refresh()
    }
    tm.turn()
}
```

When you load that sample in the browser, you'll see a dungeon with a player character in the room at the top-left corner, just like Figure 3-4. You can use the arrow keys to move the character around. Holding a key pressed will slowly move the character in that direction, thanks to our debouncing code. You'll collide with walls, and you can save some movement points by moving diagonally by pressing both arrow keys at the same time as the turn() code checks for all of the inputs in a single iteration.

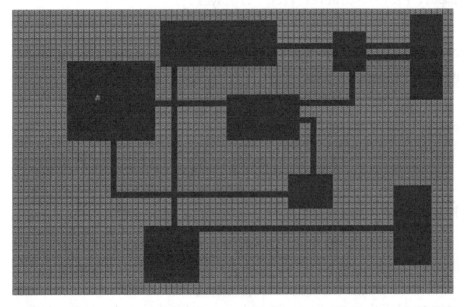

Figure 3-4. Playable dungeon

Exercise

Can you alter the player class so that it has more moves per turn? Can you make the player dig through walls?

Summary

This chapter finally started us in the journey of roguelike development. You worked hard and now you have both a dungeon and a moving character. Let us recap what we've learned:

- How to use Phaser scene lifecycle functions such as `preload()`, `create()`, and `update()` in a roguelike development setting

- How to implement turn-based mechanics on top of a genre-agnostic game development library

- What tilemaps are and how to use them

Study and get to know the final sample well; we'll be using and improving upon the dungeon and the turn manager modules and the player class because in the next chapter, we're adding monsters.

CHAPTER 4

Enemies and Permadeath

Before we start to work on enemies and combat mechanics, we're going to do a large refactor of our codebase. This will make it easier to work with multiple game entities such as enemies and monsters and introduce some new features from Phaser.

The new dungeon module will have more responsibilities than before as it will be used to manage both the level rendering and the game entity movements. Previously, our player class would change the dynamic layer tilemap directly when it needed to move. After our refactor, that class will call the functions provided by the dungeon module to move. The objective is to make it easier to develop the monster classes afterward; if every game entity class was probing and changing the tilemap directly, it would be quite hard to maintain the game code as any alteration would probably span multiple classes.

The source code for the first sample used in this chapter is at `chapter-4/example-1-tween-movement/`.

© Andre Alves Garzia 2020
A. A. Garzia, *Roguelike Development with JavaScript*,
https://doi.org/10.1007/978-1-4842-6059-3_4

Dungeon initialization

The initialization function for the dungeon remains largely the same; we just moved some variables around to make them easier to access by other functions. The new initialize function looks like

```
initialize: function (scene) {
    this.scene = scene
    this.level = level
    let levelWithTiles = level.map(r => {
        return r.map(t => {
            return t == 1 ? this.sprites.wall : ↵
            this.sprites.floor
        })
    })

    const config = {
        data: levelWithTiles,
        tileWidth: this.tileSize,
        tileHeight: this.tileSize,
    }
    const map = scene.make.tilemap(config)
    const tileset = map.addTilesetImage('tiles', 'tiles', ↵
    this.tileSize, this.tileSize, 0, 1)
    this.map = map.createDynamicLayer(0, tileset, 0, 0)

}
```

It is largely unchanged; we just moved some variables to be a part of the dungeon object. At the end of this function, we have the following properties set:

- `dungeon.scene`: Which stores a reference to the Phaser scene

- `dungeon.map`: Which stores a reference to the Phaser dynamic layer used for the ground tiles

- `dungeon.level`: Which stores a reference to the original array used for the level data

The major additions to the dungeon module are related to game entity movement, and those are what we're doing next.

Movement support

In the previous chapter, the player was just a tile on the tilemap, and movement happened by flipping the destination tile with the player and the original position into a floor tile. We'll refactor that as well and change the player to use sprites.[1] The reason for this refactor is that sprites can be animated with tweens, and we'll switch to using those for our movement.

Sprites are free-floating game objects that are placed in the game world. Usually game entities like the player character, enemies, bullets, and other objects that the player interact with or are moving in the scenery are all usually done with sprites in 2D games.

As mentioned before, all of this is just to be able to use tweens. You might have noticed that the player movement in the previous chapter was a bit clunky. The player character basically teleported from their original position to the final position. Normally, this doesn't bother much because that teleportation is on the player character and a consequence of player input, so you're usually looking at the character and interacting with it, and so even if the movement is instantaneous and clunky, it is a movement

---

[1]Phaser sprite documentation: `https://photonstorm.github.io/phaser3-docs/ Phaser.GameObjects.Sprite.html`

61

that you're expecting. Once we start adding enemy game entities, this kind of behavior becomes way less desirable. You don't want your player pondering which monsters moved because the movement didn't contain enough visual feedback to draw their attention to it.

Tweens allow us to manipulate properties of game objects over time. We'll use them to manipulate the position of the game entity from a tile to the next over some milliseconds. Instead of instantly teleporting between tiles, the player character will move from one tile to the other.

There is an important disconnection that we must take into account though. Our mental model for the roguelike is a square grid that represents a dungeon and in which monsters and the player are placed. The level array stores this representation, but as explained earlier, we'll have a dynamic layer with sprites floating on top of it, which is a different way of displaying what is actually happening inside the level array. Because of that, the movement functions we're about to implement will act on sprites and tweens but take into account the data from level.

Initializing entities

Just like there is an initialize function for the level, we'll implement a function called initializeEntity to set up the sprite for a given entity and add it to the dungeon. This function will be called by the constructors of our game entities.

```
initializeEntity: function(entity) {
    let x = this.map.tileToWorldX(entity.x)
    let y = this.map.tileToWorldY(entity.y)
    entity.sprite = this.scene.add.sprite(x, y, "tiles", ↵
    entity.tile)
    entity.sprite.setOrigin(0)
}
```

The function receives a game entity and uses `tileToWorldX` which is a function from the dynamic layer to convert a coordinate from the tilemap grid into an absolute pixel-based coordinate to be used by the sprites as they float above the dynamic layer. For example, if the player was in the 2x1 position in the grid, that would actually be the 16x0 coordinate in pixels. The dynamic map knows the size of each tile and uses that in the conversion between tile coordinates and world coordinates.

Next, we add a new property to the entity; we call it sprite and it holds a reference to the sprite being created. The code is very similar to the code used in Chapter 2 to add text to the screen. Phaser is quite consistent with its `scene.add.*` methods. The first two arguments are the position where the sprite should be placed. The third and fourth arguments are the width and height in pixels of the sprite. The fifth is the spritesheet, and the last is which tile you want to use. You might have noticed that the tile is coming from `entity.tile` and that in the previous chapter we called the reference to the tile `entity.sprite`; we'll change that once we refactor the player in the next section.

Moving entities

To move an entity, we'll need the entity and the final position where it should go. A tween will be created to animate that change of coordinates over time as can be seen in the following code:

```
moveEntityTo: function(entity, x, y) {
    entity.moving = true

    this.scene.tweens.add({
        targets: entity.sprite,
        onComplete: () => {
            entity.moving = false
            entity.x = x
            entity.y = y
        },
```

63

```
    x: this.map.tileToWorldX(x),
    y: this.map.tileToWorldY(y),
    ease: "Power2",
    duration: 200
  })
}
```

The moveEntityTo function stores a new property on the entity which holds the information if it is moving or not. This will be used later in the player class over function to decide if the turn is over or not.

All scenes come with a tween manager in scene.tweens.*[2] making it very convenient to use them. The function scene.tweens.add is used to add the tween responsible for animating the entity movement. It receives a single argument which is a configuration object describing the tween.[3] Those configurations can be very flexible, allowing you very specific control of what should happen. Our tween is very simple, just animate the change of coordinates over time. The properties used in that configuration object are

- target: A reference to which sprites are being tweened.

- onComplete: A function to be executed once the tween finishes. It is used to change entity.moving to false and to save the destination coordinates as the current coordinates for the game entity. This way, the entity position just changes once the tween ends as the entity coordinates and the sprite coordinates are not bound to each other.

---

[2]Phaser scene tweens documentation: https://photonstorm.github.io/phaser3-docs/Phaser.Tweens.TweenManager.html

[3]Tween builder configuration object documentation: https://photonstorm.github.io/phaser3-docs/Phaser.Types.Tweens.html#.TweenBuilderConfig

- x and y: The final coordinates for the sprite.

- ease: The function used to animate that transition. The function chosen is pleasing to the eye.

- duration: How long the tween should take in milliseconds.

There are no checks in this function to verify if the game entity is walking through walls or if the movement is illegal in any form. This is intentional as each game entity class might have different ways of verifying what constitutes a legal move. For example, you could create a ghost that actually walks through walls.

Still, we need to provide an easy function for the game entity classes to check if a coordinate is a walkable tile or not.

```
isWalkableTile: function (x, y) {
    return level[y][x] !== 1
}
```

It is a simple function that checks our original level array to see if the tile is a wall. With those functions in place, we can refactor the player class.

The player becomes a sprite

The changes to the player class are quite minimal but spread over most of the methods in the class. The first change needed is to make sure the constructor uses the new initializeEntity function.

```
constructor(x, y) {
    this.movementPoints = 1
    this.cursors = dungeon.scene.input.keyboard. ↵
    createCursorKeys()
    this.x = x
```

```
    this.y = y
    this.tile = 29
    this.hp = 10
    this.moving = false

    dungeon.initializeEntity(this)
}
```

There are only two changes; we renamed the property holding the value for the tile to be used for the player character from sprite to tile, as the sprite property will now be used to hold a reference to the sprite created by `initializeEntity`, which is called at the end of the constructor. In the previous version of this class, at the end, it manipulated the dynamic layer directly, making it tightly coupled with the map implementation; the new code is easier to maintain and provides the necessary separation of concerns.

Tweens are going to be used for movement, and we know from the previous section that they save a property called `moving` to flag if the game entity is moving or not. The `over` method should take that into account; we don't want our game entity passing the turn before it stops moving.

```
over() {
    return this.movementPoints == 0 && !this.moving
}
```

Even though the sprite being used for the player will have its own coordinates, they are not the same as the game entity's own coordinates which are expressed in terms of our grid system. As explained in the `onComplete` callback used by the movement tween, the final position for a movement is only set once the tween ends, and since the turn is also only over once the player stops moving, that doesn't cause a race condition. This means that in the `turn` method, which is the one used to handle movement, we shouldn't go on setting the player's coordinates in response to the cursor keys being pressed. What we need to do is to figure out where the player wants to go, check if it is a legal movement, and use moveEntityTo to move the player character there and update the coordinates.

```
turn() {

    let moved = false
    let newX = this.x
    let newY = this.y

    if (this.movementPoints > 0 && !this.moving) {
        if (this.cursors.left.isDown) {
            newX -= 1
            moved = true
        }

        if (this.cursors.right.isDown) {
            newX += 1
            moved = true
        }

        if (this.cursors.up.isDown) {
            newY -= 1
            moved = true
        }

        if (this.cursors.down.isDown) {
            newY += 1
            moved = true
        }

        if (moved) {
            this.movementPoints -= 1
```

```
        if (dungeon.isWalkableTile(newX, newY)) {
            dungeon.moveEntityTo(this, newX, newY)
        }
    }

  }
}
```

Most of this function remains the same, but instead of setting this.x and this.y directly like the previous chapter sample, we're setting two new variables newX and newY which will be passed as arguments to the moveEntityTo function later. Instead of inspecting the map data directly, the isWalkableTile function is used to figure out if the movement is legal or not.

We could be done now and just run the sample, but there is a final refactor needed. In the previous chapter, we introduced a naïve debounce function to the turn manager to prevent the player from causing multiple turns to pass in a blink of an eye as Phaser is running really fast. Since our entity will not pass the turn until the tween is over, we can remove that debouncing code and adjust the tween duration if we think the game is moving too fast.

Refactoring the turn manager is a good opportunity to go beyond just removing the debounce code. We are also replacing that loop we had in the previous sample with a better solution by holding the index of the current active entity in tm.currentIndex and advancing that once that entity's turn is over.

```
const tm = {
    entities: new Set(),
    addEntity: (entity) => tm.entities.add(entity),
    removeEntity: (entity) => tm.entities.remove(entity),
    refresh: () => {
        tm.entities.forEach(e => e.refresh())
        tm.currentIndex = 0
    },
```

```
    currentIndex: 0,
    turn: () => {
        if (tm.entities.size > 0) {
            let entities = [...tm.entities]
            let e = entities[tm.currentIndex]

            if (!e.over()) {
                e.turn()
            } else {
                tm.currentIndex++
            }
        }
    },
    over: () => [...tm.entities].every(e => e.over()),
}

export default tm
```

Gone are the code for storing the last call and the math to figure out if a given interval has passed. The turn manager code is much more straightforward now, and the game speed becomes a byproduct of the tweens used.

Now is the time to load that sample in your browser; it will look the same as the previous chapter sample until you move the player character, and then you'll notice how smooth it moves from tile to tile, leading to a much more pleasant experience.

In my opinion, that dungeon feels quite comfy, and it is time to introduce some danger to it. It is time to add a monster.

Our first monster

For this sample, we'll create and add a monster to the dungeon. It will just pursue the player character; we'll add combat in the next sample. This sample is located at chapter-4/example-2-first-monster/.

Instead of programming our own pathfinding algorithm, we're going to use the well-established A*[4] search algorithm. This is a very common algorithm that is used by many games to find a good path between two game entities. To make our work easier, we're going to use a freely available A* implementation[5] called *PathFinding.js* by Xueqiao Xu. That library is bundled with our source code inside the assets/ folder and is linked by the HTML for this sample.

```
<!DOCTYPE html>
<head>
    <title>Chapter 4 - Example 2 - First Monster</title>
    <script src="assets/phaser.js"></script>
    <script src="assets/pathfinding-browser.js"></script>
</head>

<body>
    <div id="game"></div>
    <script src="game.js" type="module"></script>
</body>

</html>
```

Since that library is included by the HTML, we don't need to use import to load it when building the monster. The *PathFinding.js* will be available as a global variable called PF.

---

[4]A* algorithm: https://en.wikipedia.org/wiki/A*_search_algorithm
[5]PathFinding.js: https://github.com/qiao/PathFinding.js

Creating the basic monster class

The code for the monster is the file monster.js, and it is very similar to the player character class. Just like all the other game entity classes we'll build, they have the turn, over, and refresh methods that are called by the turn manager.

```
import dungeon from "./dungeon.js"

export default class BasicMonster {
    constructor(x, y) {
        this.movementPoints = 1
        this.x = x
        this.y = y
        this.tile = 26
        dungeon.initializeEntity(this)
    }
}
```

Our basic monster uses the 26th tile in the spritesheet for its image and walks at the same speed as the player. The refresh and over are exactly the same as the player class.

```
refresh() {
    this.movementPoints = 1
}

over() {
    return this.movementPoints == 0 && !this.moving
}
```

This makes the monster walk one square per turn, which is a decent pace. Once you have this sample running, try experimenting with different values for refresh and the initial movement points. If you start with a large value, the monster will do a sprint on its first turn, as the turn call will repeat until the value reaches zero; if the points added during refresh are larger, then the monster will walk faster than the player, an effect that will add a lot of tension.

Moving the monster in the turn method requires a bit of explanation of how the *PathFinding.js* library works. Before attempting to find a path between two entities, you need a grid and a finder.

The *grid* is the library's representation of the level data from our game. Sometimes this grid doesn't match the same data structure as the level data, but fortunately for us, I've used the exact same data structure they use, and we can simply pass our level data to the function that creates a grid. The grid can use an array of arrays representing a square grid where 0 stands for a walkable area and 1 for a blocked area.

This library comes with many pathfinding algorithms; we'll be using A* but we could use something else. Maybe for the other monsters, we'll experiment with different pathfinding algorithms. When you create a *finder*, you specify which algorithm it is supposed to use.

Once you have these two objects created, you can use the pathfinding function to retrieve a path between the two entities. The returned value is an array containing steps, square by square, that go from the monster position to the player position.

```
turn() {
    let oldX = this.x
    let oldY = this.y

    if (this.movementPoints > 0) {
        let pX = dungeon.player.x
        let pY = dungeon.player.y
        let grid = new PF.Grid(dungeon.level)
        let finder = new PF.AStarFinder()
        let path = finder.findPath(oldX, oldY, pX, pY, grid)
```

```
    if (path.length > 2) {
        dungeon.moveEntityTo(this, path[1][0], path[1][1])
    }

    this.movementPoints -= 1
  }
}
```

The code is quite similar to the player class as is the rest of the methods as well; the main change is that instead of inspecting the cursor keys and deciding on a position, the monster uses the pathfinding library to create a grid and a finder and attempt to find a path between itself and the player. The check to see if the path array contains more than two elements is because it will include both the monster and the player position, so if it has two elements, it means the monster is next to the player and doesn't need to move.

Adding the monster to the dungeon

To add the monster to the dungeon, we'll alter the game.js file. The changes needed are quite simple; in the create function, just after adding the player to the turn manager, we'll add the monster.

We must first import the new monster class at the top of the file.

```
import BasicMonster from "./monster.js"
```

And then alter the create function.

```
create: function () {
    dungeon.initialize(this)
    dungeon.player = new PlayerCharacter(15, 15)
    tm.addEntity(dungeon.player)
    tm.addEntity(new BasicMonster(70, 8))
}
```

There is a single change, which is the final line that adds a new monster to the turn manager. You can experiment with duplicating that line a couple times and changing the coordinates to add multiple monsters to the dungeon.

You're ready to run this sample. Once loaded, it should look like Figure 4-1.

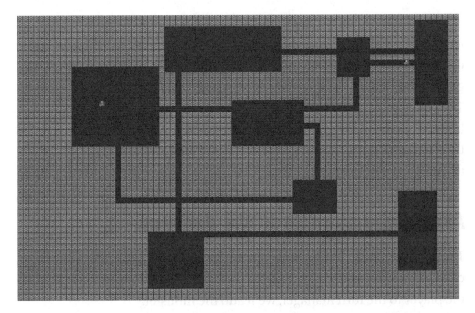

Figure 4-1. Basic monster

The little skeleton monster is on the top-right corner and will move after the player moves. It will keep trying to reach the player position. You can try escaping, but there is nowhere to run. Run around for a bit; try to see how long you can evade the skeleton. Experiment with adding multiple monsters or changing the amount of movement points they have.

In the next section, we're adding combat features.

Basic combat mechanics

To do proper combat mechanics, we need to add much more to our little sample as there is no way to know any of the stats of the player or enemies at the moment. That step will come in the next chapter as we explore treasures and upgrades, both of which also require a better user interface. For this section, we'll focus on attacking and causing damage only. The sample for this section is inside chapter-4/example-3-basic-combat/.

Just like with movement, we'll add action points to our game entities. Every turn if they have action points left, they will be able to attack another entity in range. By defining a range for the attack now, we're laying the groundwork necessary to add different weapons and magic later (and terrifying monsters). We'll also need to add some form of life meter to keep track of how much damage an entity can take before being removed from the game.

From basic monster to dangerous monster

It is more fun if we do the monster first. We need to alter all its methods so that we take into account the new properties that are used to keep track of combat-related features. By altering the monster first, and then doing the necessary refactor in the other files, we're approaching this with a top-down design method. We code for the API we want and then implement it later.

Let's begin by changing the monster constructor in monster.js.

```
constructor(x, y) {
    this.name = "A Dangerous Monster"
    this.movementPoints = 1
    this.actionPoints = 1
    this.healthPoints = 1
    this.x = x
```

```
    this.y = y
    this.tile = 26
    dungeon.initializeEntity(this)
}
```

Many new properties were added to the monster. Adding a name makes it easier for when we change the UI later. The other two properties – `actionPoints` and `healthPoints` – track how many actions, or attacks, the entity can do in one turn and how much damage it can take before it is destroyed.

Both `refresh` and `over` need to take the new properties into account so that the monster will not pass its turn before its actions are done.

```
refresh() {
    this.movementPoints = 1
    this.actionPoints = 1
}

over() {
    return this.movementPoints == 0 && this.actionPoints == ↵
    0 && !this.moving
}
```

Altering the `actionPoints` value in the `refresh` method can make the monster have more than one attack per turn; this can add a lot of tension to the game. Instead of using a property for the damage dealt by a monster attack, we're going to use a function so that it becomes easier to code different values and emulate a dice roll later. The value returned by that function is the amount of damage inflicted by the monster attack on the player.

```
attack() {
    return 1
}
```

It is important to add a little callback function for when the monster is killed. We don't have use for it yet, but we'll use it to log information to the browser console. That function will be called automatically (and so will attack) by the dungeon manager once a combat is in play.

```
onDestroy() {
    console.log(`${this.name} was killed`)
}
```

As you might have guessed, the largest change is actually to the turn function. Besides movement, it will need to keep track of how many actionPoints there are left and attack the player if it is close enough. The functions used there that are coming from the dungeon module will be implemented in the next section; don't worry, we're coding for the API we want, and later we'll make that API a reality.

```
turn() {
    let oldX = this.x
    let oldY = this.y
    let pX = dungeon.player.x
    let pY = dungeon.player.y
    let grid = new PF.Grid(dungeon.level)
    let finder = new PF.AStarFinder()
    let path = finder.findPath(oldX, oldY, pX, pY, grid)

    if (this.movementPoints > 0) {
        if (path.length > 2) {
            dungeon.moveEntityTo(this, path[1][0], path[1][1])
        }

        this.movementPoints -= 1
    }
```

```
if (this.actionPoints > 0) {
    if (dungeon.distanceBetweenEntities(this, ⏎
    dungeon.player) <= 2) {
        dungeon.attackEntity(this, dungeon.player)
    }

    this.actionPoints -= 1

  }
}
```

The beginning of this code is the part that handles movement and is already familiar to us. At the end, there is a final if clause that checks if there are actionPoints left, then checks the distance between the monster and the player (in square units) and, depending on how close they are, attacks the player.

Since this attack code is after the movement code, it means that in a single turn, the monster can walk closer to the player and then attack. If it was the other way around, the player would have a chance to get away as the movement would happen last. Switching those clauses around allows you to create very different monsters. You could, for example, have a monster with a very powerful attack, but attacking before moving. The player would be able to avoid such attack by making sure the monster doesn't start the turn near them. Part of the fun of programming roguelikes is devising nice mechanics for the player to discover and start thinking tactically around them.

Before we're able to test this out, we must implement the missing functions.

Refactoring the dungeon manager

There are many changes needed to add support for combat in the dungeon manager. One of the most important changes is that the dungeon manager needs to be aware of which entities are on the scene, which means it needs access to the turn manager. Up until now, those two modules have been completely independent, and you could in theory replace them with completely different mechanics, such as making an action roguelike instead of a turn-based one, by simply altering the turn manager.

After this chapter, these two modules will remain quite independent of each other, but the dungeon module will access the *entities set* from the turn manager to get entities when it needs to compute the distance between them and to calculate if a tile is walkable or not (gone are the days of walking over monsters).

Because of that, we must import the turn manager at the beginning of the dungeon module, which is in dungeon.js.

```
import level from "./level.js"
import tm from "./turnManager.js"
```

The function to calculate if a tile is walkable or not must be changed to take into account all the entity positions. We don't want monsters and the player walking over each other.

```
isWalkableTile: function (x, y) {
    // check all entities.
    let allEntities = [...tm.entities]
    for (let e = 0; e < allEntities.length; e++ ) {
        let entity = allEntities[e]
        if (entity.x == x && entity.y == y) {
            return false
        }
    }
    // check level
    let tileAtDestination = dungeon.map.getTileAt(x, y)
    return tileAtDestination.index !== dungeon.sprites.wall
}
```

There are two checks in the function now. The first one loops all the entities trying to match if the entity coordinate is the same as the arguments used to call the function. If they are, then that tile is not walkable. The second check is the one we had before which checks the value of the tile at the location.

Be aware that monsters don't use this function, so they are still able to walk over each other. This function is only used by the player and prevents the player from walking through the monsters. A side effect from this change is that monsters can now corner the player, and unless the player is able to kill any of the monsters, they will be trapped and suffering damage every turn. If you don't want that, you can remove that first check and allow the player to pass through (and occupy) the same tiles as the monsters.

An important aspect from that function is that it returns a Boolean, which means that even though the player class will know that it can't walk into some position, it has no way of knowing if that position is occupied by a wall or a game entity. To solve that, we're implementing the entityAtTile function which returns the entity at a given tile or `false`.

```
entityAtTile: function (x, y) {
    let allEntities = [...tm.entities]
    for (let e = 0; e < allEntities.length; e++ ) {
        let entity = allEntities[e]
        if (entity.x == x && entity.y == y) {
            return entity
        }
    }
    return false
}
```

It is a variation of the isWalkableTile, but instead of returning just a Boolean, it returns the entity that occupies that tile. Both functions could be combined into a function that worked backward, something like an isBlockedTile that returned the entity or false, and then the player class could use a Boolean negation operator to check if they can move into that space or not. I decided against doing it that way because the code becomes more opaque. This code may contain more duplication, but it is easier to understand and refactor, two qualities that are very important in a game.

The monster class uses distanceBetweenEntities to find out if the player is close enough; let's implement that.

```
distanceBetweenEntities: function(e1, e2) {
    let grid = new PF.Grid(dungeon.level)
    let finder = new PF.AStarFinder({
        allowDiagonal: true
    })
    let path = finder.findPath(e1.x, e1.y, e2.x, e2.y, grid)
    if (path.length >= 2) {
        return path.length
    } else {
        return false
    }
}
```

This code is very similar to the movement code used in the monster class. The main difference is that the finder is being initialized with support for diagonal movement. Our monster can't walk in a diagonal, but the player can; this provides a tactical advantage for the player if they need to get away from the monster as each square they move in a diagonal causes the monster to waste two moves. If the distance calculation didn't use diagonal movement to compute the path, you end up with strange values depending on the entity position; they'd appear to be two squares away, but the function would report them being three squares away.

Playing with allowing diagonal movement, different refresh rates for the points, and variadic damage results allows you to create monsters who feel very different from one another. Imagine, for example, a *vampire lord*; it would remain on its chamber until the player comes 15 squares from it, and then it awakes; after that, it moves three squares per turn and does a ton of attacks per turn. Can you implement that?

The logical function to implement next is the `attackEntity`. The essence of that function is quite simple to understand; it needs to call the attacker's `attack` method and subtract that value from the `healthPoints` of the entity being attacked.

Much like the movement function, the game becomes better if we add some visual feedback to the attack action. Because of that, there will be a tween in that function; it will move the attacker to the victim's tile and back to its original tile very quickly.

There is a chance that the attacker is moving already when `attackEntity` is called; by moving I mean that there is a tween already happening whose target is the attacker. This can happen if the attacker just moved or if the attacker has multiple attacks per turn and is already attacking. There will be some math in that function to keep track of what is going on and add some delays to the tweens so they don't overlap much.

Most of the actual combat-related part of the code will be handled in the `onComplete` callback of the tween, so it happens after the animation. The code out of it is just a complex way of calculating the delay for the tween itself so that it doesn't overlap with others.

Since this tween needs to move into the victim tile and back, we're using a property called `yoyo`; this is a Boolean that causes the tween to be repeated in reverse once it completes.

The `hold` property is how many milliseconds the tween should remain in position before repeating or yo-yoing back.

`duration` and `delay` are self-explanatory; they mean how quick should it all happen and how long should the tween manager wait before starting the tween.

```
attackEntity: function(attacker, victim) {
    attacker.moving = true
    attacker.tweens = attacker.tweens || 0
    attacker.tweens += 1

    this.scene.tweens.add({
        targets: attacker.sprite,
        onComplete: () => {
            attacker.sprite.x = this.map.tileToWorldX(attacker.x)
            attacker.sprite.y = this.map.tileToWorldX(attacker.y)
            attacker.moving = false
            attacker.tweens -= 1

            let damage = attacker.attack()
            victim.healthPoints -= damage

            console.log(`${attacker.name} does ${damage} ↵
            damage to ${victim.name} which now has ↵
            ${victim.healthPoints} life left`)

            if (victim.healthPoints <= 0) {
                this.removeEntity(victim)
            }
        },
        x: this.map.tileToWorldX(victim.x),
        y: this.map.tileToWorldY(victim.y),
        ease: "Power2",
        hold: 20,
        duration: 80,
        delay: attacker.tweens * 200,
        yoyo: true
    })
}
```

There is a lot going on inside onComplete. Let's unpack it piece by piece. The initial block manages the tween count and the moving flag, so that the entity is marked as stationary, and its tween count is diminished so that it eventually returns to zero once all the tweens complete.

Another important part of that block is that it sets the sprite coordinates back to what they should be. That tween will move the sprite to the victim's tile location and back to the position the sprite was when the tween started; so if by any reason the tweens end up overlapping each other, the start position for the tween will not be the position where the sprite should originally be located, causing that sprite to be at the wrong position when the tween ends. Resetting that value is crucial to align the sprite to the grid at the end of the animation.

The next block, which actually gets the damage and applies it to the victim, is very straightforward. What comes after it is something we haven't used before, a simple console.log call to output some data about the attack. We're doing that because we don't have a better UI yet, and we want to know what's going on.

At the end of the onComplete callback, there is a check to see if the healthPoints for the victim are over and remove it from the game. There is a chance that after an attack, the healthPoints for the victim will reach negative values, so we need to be careful there. During some initial tests here, I made an immortal skeleton, because I was checking for the healthPoints to be exactly zero and my skeleton health reached negative values, that even though quite appropriate for an undead monster, made for a relentless and impossible-to-kill adversary.

If the entity is killed, then it must be removed; let's implement the removeEntity function next.

```
removeEntity: function(entity) {
    tm.entities.delete(entity)
    entity.sprite.destroy()
    entity.onDestroy()
}
```

To understand that function, we need to remember that there are two representations of each game entity loaded in the game. There is the sprite who is floating above the dynamic map and the game entity instance that is added to the turn manager. Removing an entity from the game thus means removing it from both places and calling the instance's onDestroy method (in case it needs to do any cleanup or output some message). Once the entity is not tied to any live data structure, it will be collected by the JS garbage collector.

If you'd start the sample with just these changes, it would be a very challenging game as the player has no way to attack the monsters. It is time to change that by refactoring the player class.

The player class learns how to attack

The changes to the player class resemble the ones done for the monster class. After all, our game entities are all cut from the same cloth. The new constructor fills up the same properties that we set for the monster but with different values to make the player a bit harder to kill.

```
constructor(x, y) {
    this.name = "The Player"
    this.movementPoints = 1
    this.actionPoints = 1
    this.healthPoints = 15
    this.cursors = dungeon.scene.input.keyboard.createCursorKeys()
    this.x = x
    this.y = y
    this.tile = 29
    this.moving = false

    dungeon.initializeEntity(this)
}
```

The `refresh` function is the same as the monster class and just fills the `actionPoints` and `movementPoints` back up.

```
refresh() {
    this.movementPoints = 1
    this.actionPoints = 1
}
```

An important difference between the player and the monster class is that, if you notice closely, the monster spends their `movementPoints` and `actionPoints` regardless if they moved or attacked; this is done so that they pass their turn if they don't have anyone to attack or no movement to make. It is a simplistic way of solving it, but it works.

The player on the other hand doesn't need such check; the over check for the player remains the same as the previous sample, just checking to see if the player is moving and that their `movementPoints` are spent. The player attacks by moving, so if there is no movement attempt, there is no attack.

We're adding an `onDestroy` callback that reloads the page if the player is killed, a poor man's way of restarting the game, and an `attack` function just like the monster class.

Roguelikes often feature permadeath; this means that once the player dies, the game restarts with a whole new experience. We're not doing procedural generation yet, so our restart once the player dies leads to the exact same experience. Still, if the player dies and the game is restarted, they will need to kill all the enemies again. When we start with procedural generation, permadeath will have a totally different feel.

```
attack() {
    return 1
}

onDestroy() {
    alert("OMG! you died!")
    location.reload()
}
```

As expected, the largest change is to the turn function. The way attacks work for the player is that if it attempts to move into a blocked tile, and that tile happens to contain an entity, then the player attacks that entity.

```
turn() {
    let oldX = this.x
    let oldY = this.y
    let moved = false
    let newX = this.x
    let newY = this.y

    if (this.movementPoints > 0) {
        if (this.cursors.left.isDown) {
            newX -= 1
            moved = true
        }

        if (this.cursors.right.isDown) {
            newX += 1
            moved = true
        }

        if (this.cursors.up.isDown) {
            newY -= 1
            moved = true
        }

        if (this.cursors.down.isDown) {
            newY += 1
            moved = true
        }

        if (moved) {
            this.movementPoints -= 1
```

```
            if (!dungeon.isWalkableTile(newX, newY)) {
                let enemy = dungeon.entityAtTile(newX, newY)

                if (enemy && this.actionPoints > 0) {
                    dungeon.attackEntity(this, enemy)
                    this.actionPoints -= 1
                }

                newX = oldX
                newY = oldY
            }
            if (newX !== oldX || newY !== oldY) {
                dungeon.moveEntityTo(this, newX, newY)
            }
        }
    }

    if (this.healthPoints <= 5) {
        this.sprite.tint = Phaser.Display.Color.GetColor(255,0,0)
    }
}
```

The movement code is not really changed from the last sample. It
still checks each cursor key and produces a pair of newX and newY that
represents where the player is attempting to go. What is different is that if it
is a blocked tile, we attempt to get which entity is occupying that tile with a
call entityAtTile. If the returned value is an entity (and thus not false),
the player uses attackEntity to attack it.

A little addition is the final if clause that checks how much
healthPoints the player has left; and if the amount is below a threshold, it
colors the player sprite red to show it is in danger.

You could, in the refresh callback, add some healthPoints back to the
player, so that they heal over time.

With those changes in place, you can load the sample and attempt to kill the monster. It is more fun to go back to game.js and add some more monsters to ramp up the difficulty. In Figure 4-2, you can see the result of adding more monsters to the dungeon and trying to fight it out. I've added the output from the console to this screenshot so that we get a better idea of what is going on.

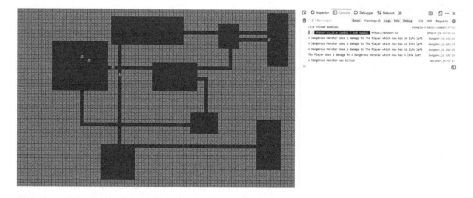

Figure 4-2. *Basic combat*

Exercises

This chapter has great opportunities for experimentation. I've been sprinkling the content with ideas, and I hope you tried some of them out. If you didn't, here are some experiments for you to implement:

- Create a new type of skeleton that moves faster but does less damage.

- Create a monster that doesn't move until the player is at 15 squares from it. Then it pursues the player and delivers a lot of damage.

- Instead of delivering always the same amount of damage, try replacing that value with a random number.

Summary

This has been a very important chapter, and it is crucial that you experiment with the code from the last sample and get a good feel about how the player and monster classes interact.

The same lifecycle methods used in the player movement – `turn`, `over`, and `refresh` – can be used to create monsters when paired with a pathfinding library.

`Sprites` give us a lot of freedom and flexibility to animate our entities using tweens and tints. We must be careful to keep the entity position in sync with the sprite position though as our game entities are now more complex than simple tiles.

Dying causes the game experience to restart, and the player loses all the progress they've made so far. This is, in my opinion, an important aspect of the roguelike experience. It makes for cautious players.

Concentrating the movement and combat handling routines in our dungeon module allows us to quickly experiment with creating new game entities and letting them loose in the dungeon. Go ahead, just release some unkillable monster that walks fast there, and play with it.

In the next chapter, we'll turn all this up to eleven with treasures, and equipment.

CHAPTER 5

Treasures and Equipment

In this chapter, we are going to learn how to add treasures and equipment to our game. These items will be game entities like our player character and the monsters and will be placed into random positions inside the dungeon.

Adding support for such items is not just a matter of creating the entities and throwing them onto the map. There needs to be some user interface to handle inventory. Before working on the items themselves, we need to work on the game UI.

Creating a user interface for our game

We've reached the point in our game development in which we need a better UI to be able to handle the features we want to add to it. To be able to create this user interface, we're going to refactor most of the files we've used so far as our game loop and game entities all need to become aware of the new UI. Once we're done with these changes, our interface will look like Figure 5-1.

© Andre Alves Garzia 2020
A. A. Garzia, *Roguelike Development with JavaScript*,
https://doi.org/10.1007/978-1-4842-6059-3_5

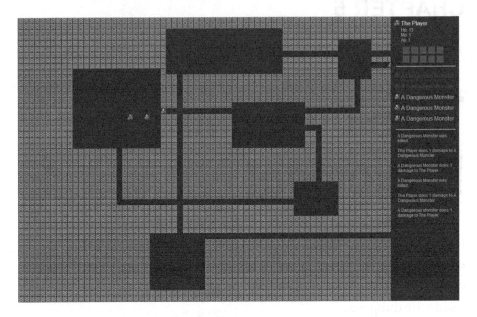

Figure 5-1. *Dungeon user interface*

The UI is based on a sidebar positioned at the right side of the screen containing three distinct regions. At the top, there is information about the player, listing the following items:

- The sprite image for the player along with its name

- Health points

- Movement points

- Action points

- Ten slots for inventory

Following that section is just a list of the monsters in the current level. As the monsters are killed, their entry is dimmed. I've opted not to display the monsters statistics at the moment to save space.

The last section is a text output about the recent actions in the game. It lists the interactions between the player and the monsters.

How it was implemented

In Chapter 2, we've learned about Phaser scenes.[1] To implement the UI, we'll use Phaser's feature to overlay a scene on top of another. We'll shrink the dungeon scene to free up space on the right and then overlay a UI scene on top of it, drawing only on the right side.

Each of our game entities – the monsters and the player – will receive the UI scene on a special callback function they'll all implement called createUI, which will be responsible for drawing that entity UI in the correct scene. By making each entity responsible for their own UI, we make our life easier from a maintainability point of view because we reduce the amount of files we need to touch when we decide to refactor the UI for a given entity.

As mentioned earlier, all of this is a huge change to the codebase, but it will open the doors for more complex mechanics and features. Let's begin by refactoring game.js.

The files for this first sample are in chapter-5/example-1-basic-ui.

Game.js refactoring

Up till now, we've been mixing the game bootstrapping with the world scene in the same game.js file. We're going to extract the world scene into its own file and minimize the amount of code inside the game. js bootstrapping file. The UI scene will also be placed on its own file. Both files will be imported by game.js and used in the Phaser game configuration object.

```
import ui from "./ui.js"
import world from "./world.js"
```

---

[1] Phaser scene documentation: https://photonstorm.github.io/phaser3-docs/Phaser.Scene.html

```
const config = {
    type: Phaser.AUTO,
    width: 80 * 16,
    height: 50 * 16,
    backgroundColor: "#472d3c",
    parent: "game",
    pixelArt: true,
    zoom: 1,
    scene: [world, ui],
    physics: {
        default: "arcade",
        arcade: {
            gravity: { y: 0 }
        }
    }
}

const game = new Phaser.Game(config)
```

The file became much simpler; all the extraneous code has been removed. Besides deleting a ton of lines, the biggest change is importing both scenes and loading them in the scene: [world, ui] line.

With that refactor done, it is time to work on world.js.

Implementing world.js

A large part of the new world.js is just what we removed from the previous incarnation of game.js, but there are some new parts which will be explained later in this section.

At the top of the file, let's import all the modules that are needed:

```
import dungeon from "./dungeon.js"
import tm from "./turnManager.js"
import PlayerCharacter from "./player.js"
import BasicMonster from "./monster.js"
```

The world.js file is the scene that contains all the game we've implemented so far in the book so it should be quite familiar.

```
const world = {
    key: "world-scene",
    active: true,
```

The first change is adding a key and an active flag to the scene. We pass multiple scenes in the game configuration object inside game.js. From those scenes, Phaser will only automatically load the ones which have active set to true. The key is set so that one scene can refer to the other by name.

```
    preload: function () {
        this.load.spritesheet('tiles', 'assets/colored.png',
            {
                frameWidth: 16,
                frameHeight: 16,
                spacing: 1
            })
    },
```

The preload function remains exactly the same. The important changes are in the next function which is create.

```
create: function () {
    dungeon.initialize(this)

    // Load game entities
    dungeon.player = new PlayerCharacter(15, 15)

    tm.addEntity(dungeon.player)
    tm.addEntity(new BasicMonster(20, 20))
    tm.addEntity(new BasicMonster(20, 10))
    tm.addEntity(new BasicMonster(76, 10))
    tm.addEntity(new BasicMonster(29, 24))
    tm.addEntity(new BasicMonster(29, 20))
```

The beginning for the create function initialized the dungeon and load the game entities – all very similar to what we've done before. The next section of the create function is new. It uses a Phaser scene built-in camera manager[2] to change the scene viewport so that there is free space on the right side for the UI scene to fill up.

```
    // Set camera, causes game viewport
    // to shrink on the right side freeing
    // space for the UI scene.
    let camera = this.cameras.main
    camera.setViewport(0, 0, camera.worldView.width-200, ↩
    camera.worldView.height)
    camera.setBounds(0, 0, camera.worldView.width, ↩
    camera.worldView.height)
    camera.startFollow(dungeon.player.sprite)
```

[2]Scene camera manager docs: https://photonstorm.github.io/phaser3-docs/Phaser.Cameras.Scene2D.CameraManager.html

The setViewport function is used to shrink the viewport. The setBounds limits the camera movement so that it doesn't go over the dungeon while moving. The camera moves because the startFollow function is used to make it track the player position.

```
    // Trigger UI scene construction
    this.events.emit('createUI')
},
```

Each scene comes with a built-in event manager. We're going to use events to send messages back and forth between the world and the UI scenes. The reason behind emitting an event during create is because the UI scene needs the game entities to be in place before it renders the user interface. If we simply load the two scenes in the game configuration object with active set to true, we end up with a race condition in which they're competing trying to render at the same time without having the necessary elements loaded for it to work correctly.

```
    update: function () {
        if (tm.over()) {
            tm.refresh()
        }
        tm.turn()
    }
}

export default world
```

The update function remains the same as well. At the end, we export the world object since the scene is now a JS module.

Before implementing the UI scene, let's take a brief detour to make some additions to dungeon.js.

New dungeon.js feature

In the dungeon module, there are some `console.log()` calls to output useful information to the console. That kind of text actually belongs in the game UI. To support that, we need to refactor those calls into something that the UI scene can use later.

A `msgs` array was added to the dungeon module; it will hold that textual data:

```
let dungeon = {
         msgs: [],
```

A new `log` function is used to populate that array:

```
 log: function(text) {
     this.msgs.unshift(text)
     this.msgs = this.msgs.slice(0,8)
 }
```

That function fixes the `msgs` array into holding a maximum of eight elements. The new text is inserted to the front of the array so that the player can read first what happened last.

After that, it is just a matter of tweaking the `console.log` in the attack function to use the new `log` function:

```
this.log(`${attacker.name} does ${damage} damage to ↵
${victim.name}.`)
```

It is time to build the UI scene.

Creating the UI scene

The UI scene source code is in the `ui.js` file. It is very similar to the world scene we use. It has both `create` and `update`, but it doesn't have a `preload` because the world scene will preload the tilemap used by this scene as well.

An important characteristic of this scene is that it depends on the entities being loaded into the turn manager for it to work. Since we can't guarantee that they will all be loaded by the time create starts executing, we're wrapping the part of the code that relies on entities into a callback function for a custom event which will be sent by the world scene once it finishes loading the entities into the turn manager.

The UI scene will need access to the turn manager to get the entities and to the dungeon module to get the msgs array:

```
import dungeon from "./dungeon.js"
import tm from "./turnManager.js"

const ui = {
    key: "ui-scene",
    active: true,
```

The scene has a custom key so that other parts of the source code are able to get it and is set to load at the start of the game.

A createdUI Boolean is going to be used by both create and update to figure out if the user interface has been added to the screen or not. This is necessary because update might run before the custom event arrives from the world scene; in that case, there is no UI to update yet, and it shouldn't attempt to access it.

```
create: function () {
        this.createdUI = false

        this.scene.get('world-scene').events.on('createUI', ↵
        () => {
            let iterator = tm.entities.values()
            let x = (80 * 16) - 190
            let y = 10
```

```
        for (let entity of iterator) {
            if (typeof entity.createUI === "function") {
                let height = entity.createUI({
                    scene: this,
                    x,
                    y,
                    width: 198
                })

                y += height

            }
        }

        this.add.line(x+5, y, 0, 10, 175, 10, ↵
        0xcfc6b8).setOrigin(0)

        this.log = this.add.text(x+10, y+20, "", {
            font: '12px Arial',
            color: '#cfc6b8',
            wordWrap: {
                width: 180
            }
        })

        this.createdUI = true
    })
},
```

The create function needs to add a callback for the custom event sent by the world scene. Each scene gets its own event manager. We must use the event manager from the world scene. If we simply register a callback for that event name on the UI scene event manager, it would never trigger as the events will not cross between separate event managers. To do that, we first get a reference to the scene itself – finally using those keys we set – and then use that scene event manager to register a callback. Let me repeat that line of code here so it is clearer:

```
this.scene.get('world-scene').events.on('createUI' ...
```

The content inside that callback is the user interface creation code. It relies on fetching an iterator[3] from the dungeon.entities set. A function called createUI is called for each entity. This function received a configuration object with coordinates and the width for the user interface; each entity can then decide on how much height it should use and return that amount. This value is used to compute the position for the next entity.

This way, each entity can create their own custom UI or even no interface at all and just return zero. From the point of view of the UI scene, the player and the monsters are all the same. It calls createUI for each of them and lets each entity manage its own interface. Even though this adds more code to each entity, it is more flexible in the long run, and it becomes easier to maintain as the code for each entity is self-contained.

The iterator loop might look a bit strange. Reading the documentation page referenced in the footnotes will make it a lot clearer. Basically, when iterating through values(), the value returned by the iterator is the entity.

Once all that entity UI creation is done, we add a line to be a visual separator between the entity user interfaces and the next section which is a text object to display the data in the dungeon.msgs array. After that, the UI is created, and we can set that createdUI flag to true.

---

[3]Set entries() iterator documentation: https://developer.mozilla.org/en-US/docs/Web/JavaScript/Reference/Global_Objects/Set/entries

The next step in implementing the UI scene is the update function, which is very simple, and exporting the scene.

```
update: function() {
        if (this.createdUI) {
            let text = dungeon.msgs.join(`\n\n`)
            this.log.setText(text)
        }
    }
}

export default ui
```

The dungeon.msgs array is joined with two carriage returns so that there is some visual separation between messages. The code for handling word wrapping is provided by Phaser itself. In the text object creation in the create function, we set the width for word wrapping to be 180. This will cause the text messages to fall into a nice column display on our game UI.

All that is left is to implement createUI for each entity. The UI we're using for the monster is simpler than the one for the player; let's start with that one first.

Implementing the monster UI

The monster user interface is very simple; it just shows the monster sprite and its name. One thing it does that is not clear in the book screenshots is that it changes the color of the monster name during its turn so that the player knows which monster is moving. This causes a nice effect as each monster name blinks in sequence as their turns progress until it's the player's turn again.

Let's implement the createUI function.

```
createUI(config) {
    let scene = config.scene
    let x = config.x
    let y = config.y

    this.UIsprite = scene.add.sprite(x, y, "tiles", ⏎
    this.tile).setOrigin(0)
    this.UItext = scene.add.text(x+20, y, this.name, { font: ⏎
    '16px Arial', fill: '#cfc6b8' })

    return 30
}
```

The config object contains the position and a reference to the UI scene – and the width but that is not used in this function – those values are used to position a sprite and a text.

The value returned by this function is used by the UI scene to compute the coordinates for the next entity. This allows entity user interfaces to have a flexible height.

Blinking when it is the entity's turn can be implemented by altering the over since that is the function that actually knows if the turn is over or not. Another visual effect that we'll implement is dimming the monster name when it is killed. That can be implemented in the onDestroy function.

```
over() {
    let isOver = this.movementPoints == 0 && ⏎
    this.actionPoints == 0 && !this.moving
    if (isOver && this.UItext) {
        this.UItext.setColor("#cfc6b8")
    } else {
        this.UItext.setColor("#fff")
    }
```

```
        return isOver
    }

    onDestroy() {
        dungeon.log(`${this.name} was killed.`)
        this.UIsprite.setAlpha(0.2)
        this.UItext.setAlpha(0.2)
    }
```

It is important to check if the UItext has been created because that over function might be called before the UI scene receives the custom event from the world. Depending if the turn isOver or not, we change the color of the text.

When the monster is killed, dungeon.log is used to add a message to the text display of the game, and the entity UI is dimmed by altering its opacity.

The player UI is very similar to this one, but it has more elements; let's implement it.

The player user interface

Besides a display similar to the monster UI with the sprite and name being shown, the player user interface also contains the stats and inventory slots, which are unused now but will be used by the next sample which is about equipment.

To support the new UI, we'll implement a createUI function and alter the over function so that the player name also highlights when it's their turn. We'll go over the createUI function in steps as it contains different sections.

```
    createUI(config) {
        let scene = config.scene
        let x = config.x
        let y = config.y
        let accumulatedHeight = 0
```

To make it easier to calculate the height used by the interface, we've added a variable called accumulatedHeight. As we build each section of the player UI, we'll add their heights to this variable.

```
// Character sprite and name
this.UIsprite = scene.add.sprite(x, y, "tiles", ↵
this.tile).setOrigin(0)

this.UIheader = scene.add.text(
    x + 20,
    y,
    this.name,
    {
        font: '16px Arial',
        color: '#cfc6b8'
})
```

Adding the hero sprite and its name is done in the same way as the monster user interface.

```
// Character stats
this.UIstatsText = scene.add.text(
    x + 20,
    y + 20,
    `Hp: ${this.healthPoints}\nMp: ↵
${this.movementPoints}\nAp: ${this.actionPoints}`,
    {
        font: '12px Arial',
        fill: '#cfc6b8'
})

accumulatedHeight += this.HPtext.height + ↵
this.UIsprite.height
```

The character stats is just a text with carriage returns in it. Variable interpolation using template strings[4] will add the correct values for the data into the displayed text. This text uses a smaller font size than the previous section, allowing us to display more information in less space.

Inventory display is done using empty squares. There are ten slots arranged into two rows of five elements. This number is not arbitrary; later we'll use the numbers in the keyboard to activate equipment so each slot will match a keyboard key.

```
// Inventory screen
let itemsPerRow = 5
let rows = 2
this.UIitems = []

for (let row = 1; row <= rows; row++) {
    for (let cell = 1; cell <= itemsPerRow; cell++) {
        let rx = x + (25 * cell)
        let ry = y + 50 + (25 * row)
        this.UIitems.push(
            scene.add.rectangle(rx, ry, 20, 20, ↵
            0xcfc6b8, 0.3).setOrigin(0)
        )
    }
}

accumulatedHeight += 90
```

---

[4]Template strings documentation: https://developer.mozilla.org/en-US/docs/Web/JavaScript/Reference/Template_literals

Using nested loops, a UIitems array is created containing the ten rectangles.[5] In the next sample, we'll make use of this array to replace the empty slots with equipment.

The last item in the createUI function is just a line to be used as a divider between the player UI and the other entities.

```
// Separator
scene.add.line(x+5, y+120, 0, 10, 175, 10, 0xcfc6b8).
setOrigin(0)

return accumulatedHeight
```

That takes care of all the player's user interface creation, but we still need to implement the highlight when it is their turn and also make sure that the stats display is kept up to date. Lucky for us, we can do both in the over function.

```
over() {
    let isOver = this.movementPoints == 0 && !this.moving

    if (isOver && this.UIheader) {
        this.UIheader.setColor("#cfc6b8")
    } else {
        this.UIheader.setColor("#fff")
    }

    if (this.UIstatsText) {
        this.UIstatsText.setText( `Hp: ${this.healthPoints}
        \nMp: ${this.movementPoints}\nAp:
        ${this.actionPoints}`)
    }
    return isOver
}
```

---

[5]Rectangle factory documentation: https://photonstorm.github.io/phaser3-docs/Phaser.GameObjects.GameObjectFactory.html#rectangle__anchor

It is similar to the monster version of over, but it contains an additional section to update the UIStatsText with the current values.

That concludes all the changes needed for this first example. If you run this example, you'll be able to experience the new user interface. The next sample is all about creating equipment.

Creating equipment and treasure

Equipment and treasure will be implemented the same way in this book. That might not be how a more complex roguelike does it, but it will serve the purpose of this book well. More complex games will often have specialized data structures and classes for each kind of game entity they're building. To make this book easier to understand and the code easier to experiment with, we're using a flexible class definition and making them all conform to the same interface.

Both will be new forms of game entities – like the player and monsters – but they won't move or have user interfaces. By making them game entities, they can influence the gaming experience beyond just being acquired. They will have their own version of turn and over, which means an equipment can have an effect on each turn. A good example of such effect could be a cursed sword which is very powerful but saps health points from the player every turn.

Before we can go crazy creating items, we need to work a bit more in the files we already have. Currently, we have a UI to represent items in the user possession, but we don't have the other routines needed for it.

The code for this sample is in chapter-5/example-2-equipment/; once you open it, you'll notice some new folders inside it which we're using to better organize our code. There is a folder called items which holds all the items available in the game and another one called enemies with all the enemies.

I've moved the old `monster.js` inside the `enemies` folder and renamed it `skeleton.js`; the code in `world.js` has been updated to reflect the name change.

All the game entities will now have a new property called `type` which is a string that declares what kind of entity it is. Currently, there are three types of entity – character, enemy, item – all the current game entities have been updated to set this property in their constructor. The values for `healthPoints` in all entities have been raised so that we can play more with weapons and their effects.

With that bit of rework done, we can start making changes to the `player.js` entity.

Adding item support to the player character

Most of the work needed to support items is contained in the `player.js` class. The other entities will not interact with items much, and if they do, they'll delegate that to the player. The player will collect items during the game. Carrying an item and equipping an item are separate actions. That allows us to create items like potions which upon being equipped would trigger their effect and then self-destroy.

All items being carried by the player will appear in the inventory grid we created in the previous sample; the equipped items will appear opaque and with a white border, the others will be dimmed and without border.

To equip or unequip an item, the player will press the number on the keyboard corresponding to the chosen slot. There are two rows of five slots, so the numbers go from 0 to 9 with 0 meaning the tenth slot (so it matches the sequence in the computer keyboard).

Because the player class is now much larger than before, I'll go over it in subsections so that all the code inside it becomes clearer. The next sections will be out of order in comparison with how the code is laid out on the file itself. The way I'm explaining it here is to help with understanding how it works, but the organization in the file is better for readability and maintenance.

Equipping items

When the player equips an item, we set the item's `active` property to `true`. To support this feature, we've implemented a `toggleItem` function that receives a number corresponding to a slot in the inventory and toggles that item active or not depending on its previous state.

```
toggleItem(itemNumber) {
    const item = this.items[itemNumber]
    if (item) {
        if (item.weapon) {
            this.items.forEach(i => i.active = i.weapon ? ⏎
            false : i.active)
        }
        item.active = !item.active

        if (item.active) {
            dungeon.log(`${this.name} equips ${item.name} ⏎
            :  ${item.description}.`)
            item.equip(itemNumber)
        }
    }
}
```

The first `if` clause in that function is there to make sure we're trying to toggle an item. If we attempt to pass a number that matches an empty slot, the function just exits.

We're using that function to enforce a specific game mechanic for the player. They can only equip one weapon at a time. Equipping a weapon causes all the other weapons to unequip.

If the toggle is turning something active, we use that opportunity to display some helpful text in the game UI.

Each item can also implement the `equip` function. This function will be called if the user is setting the item to active.

Removing an item from inventory

At the moment, we have two needs regarding removing items from inventory. We want to enable things such as potions – which will cause an effect and self-destruct – and items that are able to remove other items.

To support both use cases, we're going to build two different functions. The first one is removing an item by passing its slot position in the player inventory.

```
removeItem(itemNumber) {
    const item = this.items[itemNumber]

    if (item) {
        this.items.forEach(i => {
            i.UIsprite.destroy()
            delete i.UIsprite
        })
        this.items = this.items.filter(i => i !== item)
        this.refreshUI()
    }

}
```

To remove an item, we need to

- Delete the item UIsprite, which is the sprite we place on top of the UIitem rectangles that represent the inventory slots.

- Delete the UIsprite property of the item, so that the function that refreshes the user interface creates it again.

- Remove that item from the items array.

- Refresh the user interface to display the changes.

The other function we're implementing is one that removes an item by checking if some of its properties match a given value. With that function, you can, for example, build an item that removes all items that are cursed by calling it and passing *cursed* as the property and true as the value.

```
removeItemByProperty(property, value) {
    this.items.forEach(i => {
        i.UIsprite.destroy()
        delete i.UIsprite
    })
    this.items = this.items.filter(i => i[property] !== ↵
    value)
    this.refreshUI()
}
```

Changing how attacks work

At first glance, this might not look like it is related to item handling, but it is. Prior to this sample, the player's attack has been a number returned by the attack function. We're still going to return a number from that function, but now we're going to compute it differently.

A player's attack will be determined by the equipped weapon, and to make it easier to compute that, we're going to implement a handy auxiliary function to return the equipped items.

```
equippedItems() {
    return this.items.filter(i => i.active)
}
```

Now it is easy to compute the attack value for the player.

```
attack() {
    const items = this.equippedItems()
    const combineDamage = (total, item) => total + ↵
    item.damage()

    const damage = items.reduce(combineDamage, 0)
    return damage

}
```

You might be wondering what if the user has an equipped item that doesn't do any damage; well, in that case, the item damage function returns zero.

Before this sample is over, we're going to give the player an item by prefilling the items array with a sword in the constructor and toggling it active. Without that, the player would start the game without any weapon, and it is not wise to walk into a dungeon without at least a pointy stick.

Changing the constructor

There are two changes needed in the constructor to support items. We need to add an items array property and the handler for pressing numbers to equip or unequip items. The first one is quite easy.

```
    this.items = []
```

The second one is a bit more involved. It is similar to the cursor key handling. We use the scene built-in keyboard plugin[6] to register a generic keyup event handler. This event fires once the key is released; if we were triggering things on keydown, we'd get repeated events if the user kept the key pressed, which is undesirable for our use case.

Inside the event handler, we get the value of the key that was pressed. This key property is passed into the Number constructor; if the resulting value is a number, then it means that the player pressed a numerical key; if it is NaN, then they pressed something else, and we can simply ignore it.

If the pressed key was a number, then we toggle the corresponding item that matches that value.

```
dungeon.scene.input.keyboard.on("keyup", (event) => {

    let key = event.key

    if (!isNaN(Number(key))) {

        if (key == 0) {
            key = 10
        }

        this.toggleItem(key - 1)
    }

});
```

Be aware that we need to treat 0 as 10 so that the disposition of the keys on the keyboard visually matches the slots on the screen.

---

[6]Scene built-in keyboard plugin documentation: https://photonstorm.github. io/phaser3-docs/Phaser.Input.Keyboard.KeyboardPlugin.html

Refreshing the UI

With all this item manipulation going on, we need a function to synchronize what is on screen with what we actually have inside the items array. This function will be called at every turn so that the display is always up to date.

The refreshUI function needs to double check if every item in the items array has a corresponding UIsprite. This is a sprite that is placed on top of the inventory slot to represent the item. When the player picks an item, this function will find the item in the items array, notice it doesn't contain a UIsprite, and add one, thus causing the item to appear in the inventory user interface.

Another responsibility of that function is to make sure the inventory display reflects what items are equipped or not by drawing a white border around the active items.

```
refreshUI() {
    for (let i = 0; i < this.items.length; i++) {
        let item = this.items[i]
        if (!item.UIsprite) {
            let x = this.UIitems[i].x + 10
            let y = this.UIitems[i].y + 10
            item.UIsprite = this.UIscene.add.sprite(x, y, ↵
            "tiles", item.tile)
        }
        if (!item.active) {
            item.UIsprite.setAlpha(0.5)
            this.UIitems[i].setStrokeStyle()
        }
```

```
        else {
            item.UIsprite.setAlpha(1)
            this.UIitems[i].setStrokeStyle(1, 0xffffff)
        }
    }
}
```

The final piece in our player class additions is some changes to the turn function. Tiles that contain items are not walkable, but they are also not enemies; moving into a tile that has an item should pick the item, not attack it.

Patching turn

Instead of placing the whole content of the turn function, which is very long and would span more than one book page, I'll only place the changed part here. At the end of the function, we make sure we update the user interface.

```
        this.refreshUI()
```

The other change is inside the if block that handled the movement. If the user moved, we need to check if they hit an item and then grab it.

```
if (moved) {
    this.movementPoints -= 1

    if (!dungeon.isWalkableTile(newX, newY)) {
        let entity = dungeon.entityAtTile(newX, newY)

        if (entity && entity.type == "enemy" && ↵
        this.actionPoints > 0) {
            dungeon.attackEntity(this, entity)
            this.actionPoints -= 1
        }
```

```
    if (entity && entity.type == "item" && ↵
    this.actionPoints > 0) {
        this.items.push(entity)
        dungeon.itemPicked(entity)
        dungeon.log(`${this.name} picked ${entity.name}: ↵
        ${entity.description}`)
        this.actionPoints -= 1
    } else {
        newX = oldX
        newY = oldY
    }

}
if (newX !== oldX || newY !== oldY) {
    dungeon.moveEntityTo(this, newX, newY)
}
}
```

It may look complicated, but it is simpler than it looks. The first if clause inside it double checks to see if the entity at the destination tile is an enemy by checking its type property. If it is and the player has enough actionPoints, an attack is made.

The second check is to see if the entity is an item; this is also done by checking its type property. If it is, then the item is pushed into the inventory by placing it in the items array. A new function has been added to the dungeon module (more about it in a bit) that is used to remove the item from the dungeon map picked items should vanish from the map but still be present in the turn manager.

It is important to notice that picking an item and attacking an enemy affect the movement differently. You can't walk into an enemy, so doing an attack also reverts the player's position back to its original coordinates, but you can walk into an item, which causes the player to pick it up and occupy its map position.

Reworking the dungeon module

The dungeon module also needs some fixes because up until now, all the entities in the turn manager would have a representation on the map. That is no longer true as items that are picked leave the map but are still present in the turn manager (so that they may have effects every turn).

Even though this is a small detail, this causes changes on how to compute which tiles are walkable. We can't simply loop the turn manager entities, checking if the coordinates match. We must check if the entity actually has a sprite.

```
isWalkableTile: function (x, y) {
    // check all entities.
    let allEntities = [...tm.entities]
    for (let e = 0; e < allEntities.length; e++ ) {
        let entity = allEntities[e]
        if (entity.sprite && entity.x == x && entity.y == y) {
            return false
        }
    }
    // check level
    let tileAtDestination = dungeon.map.getTileAt(x, y)
    return tileAtDestination.index !== dungeon.sprites.wall
},
```

When an item is picked, we delete its entity sprite property. This makes it vanish from the map and also marks the tile as walkable.

A similar change is needed for the entityAtTile function.

```
entityAtTile: function (x, y) {
    let allEntities = [...tm.entities]
    for (let e = 0; e < allEntities.length; e++ ) {
        let entity = allEntities[e]
```

```
        if (entity.sprite && entity.x == x && entity.y == y) {
            return entity
        }
    }
    return false
},
```

Removing an entity and picking an item are two separate functions but with very similar implementations.

```
removeEntity: function(entity) {
    tm.entities.delete(entity)
    entity.sprite.destroy()
    delete entity.sprite
    entity.onDestroy()
},
itemPicked: function(entity) {
    entity.sprite.destroy()
    delete entity.sprite
},
```

The difference is that removeEntity also removes it from the turn manager and calls the entity.onDestroy function.

Initializing entities needs changing as well because we may add entities to the turn manager that will not be present in the map, such as when we start the player with some weapons already. The way to do that is just to double check if the entity has its coordinates set. Entities without coordinates are not placed on the map.

```
initializeEntity: function(entity) {
    if (entity.x && entity.y) {
        let x = this.map.tileToWorldX(entity.x)
        let y = this.map.tileToWorldY(entity.y)
```

```
        entity.sprite = this.scene.add.sprite(x, y, ↵
        "tiles", entity.tile)
        entity.sprite.setOrigin(0)
    }
  },
```

Let's create some items

We're finally ready to start pouring our creative minds into crafting some cool items for the game. All the items discussed in this section will be inside the items folder, and each item has its own file.

Items are game entities so they'll implement all the functions needed for the normal entity lifecycle such as turn, over, and refresh, but not only that, they all need to implement createUI and damage. Most items will have nothing to do inside those functions, but they need to be present because the rest of our source code assumes they're there. We could patch all the other source code to double check if those functions are present before calling them, but that would make the rest of the game harder to maintain; it is better to simply make sure the functions are present.

Still it would be quite tedious to fill every item with empty stubs for those functions. To solve that, we're creating a generic item class that implements all those functions with no-ops (aka empty functions). Our items can simply extend the generic item, and then they will just need to implement the functions they want to change.

This will make our real items more compact, and easy to understand and maintain. Let's implement the generic item class.

Implementing the generic item class

The code for this generic item class is inside the genericItem.js file inside the items folder. Even though it is an uninspiring class, it serves its purpose well, which is to save us from having to type all that boilerplate code for every single item we want to create.

```
export default class GenericItem {
    constructor(x,y) {
        this.active = false
        this.type = "item"
        this.weapon = false
        this.name = "Nameless Item"
        this.description = "it is nothing special"

        if (x && y) {
            this.x = x
            this.y = y
        }

    }

    damage() {
        return 0
    }

    turn() {

    }

    equip() {

    }

    unequip() {

    }
```

```
    refresh() {

    }

    over() {
        return true
    }

    createUI() {
        return 0
    }
}
```

Inside the constructor, there is an `if` clause checking to see if we're instantiating the item by passing coordinates or not. This is because we might want to instantiate an item not on the map but directly in the possession of the player. These items wouldn't have a coordinate as they were never in the map.

Some functions need to return values that make them have no effect in the game instead of simply not returning anything.

The `over` function needs to return true or the turn manager will be stuck waiting for the item to pass the turn forever.

Since items don't add their own UI to the game, the `createUI` should return zero height.

The same reasoning applies for the `damage` function which should return zero by default. If that function didn't return anything, an equipped item that causes no damage would cause the `attack` function to compute `NaN`.

By default, items are not weapons and are not equipped. Let's create a sword; the player is in a dangerous position without it.

Creating a sword

The code for the basic sword that the player will start the game with is inside sword.js.

```
import GenericItem from "./genericItem.js"
import dungeon from "../dungeon.js"

export default class Sword extends GenericItem {
    constructor(x, y) {
        super(x,y)
        this.tile = 994
        this.name = "A Sword"
        this.description = "A basic sword. Causes between ↵
        1 and 5 damage."
        this.weapon = true

        dungeon.initializeEntity(this)

    }

    damage() {
        return Phaser.Math.Between(1, 5)
    }
}
```

The sword is very simple. It extends the generic item class, changing some of its properties such as the tile it uses for visual representation, its name, and description, and makes sure to mark it as a weapon.

The only function it implements is the damage function. To spice things up, we're making the sword cause a random damage between 1 and 5.

Now, we need to give the player this sword at the game start by hooking it up to the player.js constructor. Import the item with

```
import Sword from "./items/sword.js"
```

And in the constructor just above the dungeon.initialize(this) function call, add

```
this.items.push(new Sword())
this.toggleItem(0)
```

That's it! The player starts the game with an equipped sword. It is not a good sword though; let's make a better one.

Creating a long sword

The code for the long sword is inside longSword.js, and it is almost the same as the sword code. It just changes how much damage it does and the associated metadata such as name, description, and tile image.

```
import GenericItem from "./genericItem.js"
import dungeon from "../dungeon.js"

export default class LongSword extends GenericItem {
    constructor(x, y) {
        super(x,y)
        this.tile = 992
        this.name = "A Long Sword"
        this.description = "A long sword that causes ↵
        between 1 and 8 damage."
        this.weapon = true

        dungeon.initializeEntity(this)

    }

    damage() {
        return Phaser.Math.Between(4, 8)
    }
}
```

We'll add this sword somewhere in the dungeon later. I bet the player will run toward it as it makes much more damage than the little knife they are given at the start.

Creating a gem

Collecting treasure as the player crawls through the dungeon is part of the game. Our gem implementation is dead simple since gems don't do anything but exist to be collected. The gem code is inside gem.js.

```
import GenericItem from "./genericItem.js"
import dungeon from "../dungeon.js"

export default class Gem extends GenericItem {
    constructor(x,y) {
        super(x,y)

        this.tile = 720
        this.name = "Gem"

        dungeon.initializeEntity(this)

    }
}
```

That gem is so useless that it doesn't even get a description. Having items that are useless by themselves can be a good part of your game design. You can have another item that has in its equip function a check to see how many useless gems the player has collected and refuses to work until a certain number is match, thus making gems some sort of fuel or lock for that item. You can also make a greedy monster that only attacks the player if they have gems in their possession. It is not because an item doesn't have any use by itself that it can't be paired with something else to provide a more memorable playing experience, so try not to think of gems, and treasure in general, as simply a game alternative to money; there are other uses for them that are more rewarding in my opinion.

In our game, we're not implementing shops or any form of game economy, so gems will only be used for pairing with some other stuff. Players might still want to collect them; they are shiny after all. So to drive a subtle argument against greediness home, let's make a cursed gem.

What about a cursed gem?

Cursed items and traps are all staples of roguelikes. In more mature games, the developers usually provide the player with some form of way to detect those items, thus rewarding the tactical player who thinks before grabbing all the shiny stuff that appears before them. We're keeping this game very minimal and are not providing any form for the player to figure out if a gem is cursed before grabbing it. Life is thought in the nano dungeon.

The code for the cursed gem is inside cursedGem.js. That item is a more complex item than the ones we've seen so far. The cursed gem is a full game entity with actionPoints and turn actions.

In each turn, it figures if the player picked it up. If it did, it activates itself, making it appear as equipped in the user interface – this is for theatrical purposes, as in equipped by itself against the player's will – and causes one point of damage every turn for the player. If the player unequips it, it will equip itself back in the next turn. It is cursed after all.

```
import GenericItem from "./genericItem.js"
import dungeon from "../dungeon.js"

export default class CursedGem extends GenericItem {
    constructor(x,y) {
        super(x,y)
        this.tile = 720
```

```
        this.name = "Cursed Gem"
        this.description = "A cursed gem that is now stuck ↵
        to your hand. You can only remove it by finding a potion."
        this.actionPoints = 1
        this.cursed = true

        dungeon.initializeEntity(this)

    }
    turn() {
        if (dungeon.player.items.includes(this)) {
            this.active = true
            dungeon.log(`Cursed gem gives 1 damage to ↵
            player. Find potion to cure.`)
            dungeon.player.healthPoints -= 1
        }

        this.actionPoints = 0
    }
    refresh() {
        this.actionPoints = 1
    }
    over() {
        return this.actionPoints == 0
    }
}
```

Much like our skeleton, the cursed gem gets one action point per turn and spends it regardless of what happens. This is a pattern that makes it act once every turn.

In each turn, it inspects the player items array looking for itself. This kind of direct inspection would be dangerous in a larger game, but our codebase is small and we can get away with it. You'd be surprised with the hacks that some larger games get away with though. It is more important that you pay attention to your game design and make your game fun to play; if you need to do some hack along the way, I'm not going to judge; it is your game, and it is marvelous.

If it finds itself in the player's possession, it damages the player and sends a message to the UI. This is necessary because without it the player might not notice they are being hit every turn. The constant text every turn also adds to the urgency in finding a cure in the form of the potion we're going to implement next.

Creating a potion

The code for the potion is inside potion.js. The potion is the cure for the cursed gem. When equipped, it will remove all the cursed items in the player possession and remove itself.

It is our first item to make use of the equip function. This function is only triggered when an item is set to active. It received the slot number in the player inventory where the item is located to make it easier to create self-destruct items by calling player.removeItem(index).

```
import GenericItem from "./genericItem.js"
import dungeon from "../dungeon.js"

export default class Potion extends GenericItem {
    constructor(x,y) {
        super(x,y)
        this.tile = 761
        this.name = "Holy Potion"
        this.description = "A potion that removes cursed ↵
        items when equipped."

        dungeon.initializeEntity(this)

    }
```

```
equip(itemNumber) {
    dungeon.log(`A blessing passes through your body and ↵
    removes all cursed items.`)
    dungeon.player.removeItemByProperty("cursed", true)
    dungeon.player.removeItem(itemNumber)
  }
}
```

As you can see, by tapping into the equip function, it is very easy to create potions. Other potions can be easily created to add more healthPoints to the player or increase the player's attack for some rounds.

Now that we have some items to play with, it is time to add them to the dungeon. We're going to do that by altering the world scene.

Adding items to the dungeon

To start using the items we just created, we must first import them at the top of the world.js file.

```
import CursedGem from "./items/cursedGem.js"
import Gem from "./items/gem.js"
import LongSword from "./items/longSword.js"
import Potion from "./items/potion.js"
```

At the same location in the create function where we add the skeleton entities, we're also going to add some items. Let me show the source code with the player and skeletons, so that it is easier to locate on the file.

```
tm.addEntity(dungeon.player)
tm.addEntity(new Skeleton(20, 20))
tm.addEntity(new Skeleton(20, 10))
tm.addEntity(new CursedGem(15, 20))
tm.addEntity(new Potion(18, 18))
tm.addEntity(new LongSword(18, 22))
```

```
tm.addEntity(new Gem(21, 21))
tm.addEntity(new Skeleton(76, 10))
tm.addEntity(new Skeleton(29, 24))
tm.addEntity(new Skeleton(29, 20))
```

You're ready to start playing with items. Once you load that sample code in your browser, you'll see a much richer map and have a more complete gaming experience as seen in Figure 5-2.

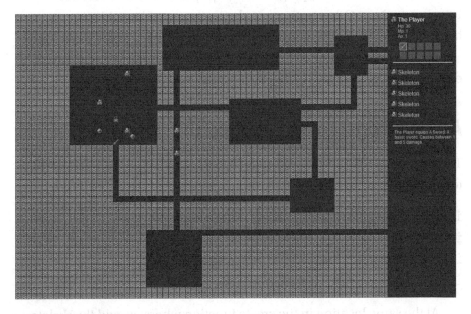

Figure 5-2. *Dungeon with items*

Adding monster loot

A common mechanic in roguelikes and RPGs is monsters dropping some items or treasure when killed. As you might have guessed already, we have all the functions we need to implement this just by adding new entities to the turn manager in the onDestroy function of a monster. The source code for this next sample is in chapter-5/example-3-loot/ folder.

The only file we're changing between the previous sample and this one is the skeleton.js source code. We want the skeleton to, maybe, drop some item when it is killed. This way the player doesn't really know if an item will be dropped and which item is going to drop.

First, let's import the items we want to have available for dropping at the top of the file. We'll also need to import the turn manager because we'll need to use it to add the dropped item to the map.

```
import Gem from "../items/gem.js"
import LongSword from "../items/longSword.js"
import Potion from "../items/potion.js"
import tm from "../turnManager.js"
```

After importing the items, we need to patch the onDestroy function.

```
onDestroy() {
    dungeon.log(`${this.name} was killed.`)
    this.UIsprite.setAlpha(0.2)
    this.UItext.setAlpha(0.2)

    // loot
    let x = this.x
    let y = this.y

    let possibleLoot = [
    false,
    false,
    Gem,
    LongSword,
    Potion
    ]
```

```
let lootIndex = Phaser.Math.Between(0,possibleLoot. ↵
length-1)
if (possibleLoot[lootIndex]) {
    let item = possibleLoot[lootIndex]
    tm.addEntity(new item(x, y))
    dungeon.log(`${this.name} drops ${item.name}.`)
}
}
```

The way loot works there is that we assemble a five-element array containing the items we want to drop and some `false` entries. A position in that array is randomized, and if it is an item instead of `false`, that item is instantiated and dropped on the map in the position that was previously occupied by the skeleton.

The reason behind having those `false` entries is so that not all kills end up turning up some loot. By adding more `false` items, we increase the probability of it not dropping anything.

In a test play here, I pressed the wrong number trying to equip a long sword and ended up using the potion before picking the cursed gem. I didn't notice that at the time and went on to pick the cursed gem just to use the potion. Then I realized what happened, and I had no potion to cure me; my only hope was to kill enough skeletons before I run out of `healthPoints` and hope one of them dropped a potion.

Exercises

There are so many tempting things to play with in this chapter that I could spend another five pages just giving you ideas to try out; instead, let me just give you three challenges:

- Can you create a health potion?

- Can you create a potion that boosts the player attacks for three rounds and then self-destructs?

- Can you create a pair of new monster and gem and make the monster only start chasing you after you pick the gem? Can you make the monster terrifying?

Summary

Our game is starting to look more like a game now. Having items and monsters allow us to start shaping the gameplay experience in more creative ways.

Before moving on to the next chapter, make sure that you

- Understand how items work inside the player class

- Understand how each of our items work

- Create some items of your own

There were a lot of complex parts involved in making the game user interface on the right side of the screen. Understanding how the scenes are overlaid on top of each other is important as well.

In the next chapter, we're going to work on new character classes for the player to use; let's keep moving.

CHAPTER 6

Character Classes

An important part of the gaming experience for many roguelikes is having multiple choices of player character archetypes available. This, I believe, comes from many of the games being inspired by tabletop role-playing games, most of which offer character classes as templates that can be used to build unique characters for each player.

In this chapter, we'll be creating character classes. This is a concept borrowed from tabletop role-playing games (TTRPGs) which you may be already familiar with through being previously exposed to these awesome games or by playing other games that featured the same concept. For the purposes of our sample game, we're treating character classes and character races as the same thing. We don't want to make this sample game too complex by offering too many combinations.

Think of classes really like archetypes. They are the common aspects that come to embody what one expects a given fictional fantasy job to be. In TTRPGs, people will often go to great lengths to customize their character and create a unique, believable, and fleshed out character. That is not what we're doing here; we're going for the archetypes, just enough aspects for it to be recognized as the archetype we want it to represent.

Before we are able to implement our classes, we'll need to refactor some of our code.

© Andre Alves Garzia 2020
A. A. Garzia, *Roguelike Development with JavaScript*,
https://doi.org/10.1007/978-1-4842-6059-3_6

Yet another refactor

It may appear that we start every single chapter with a refactor; that is true and also by design. We go from easy to understand code to more flexible and powerful constructs as the chapters fly by. In this chapter, we'll have to do yet another refactor, but before going over what needs patching, it is important to understand why we're changing the code at this point in the book.

Our hero classes will be the classical ones such as warrior, elf, dwarf, and so on. We need to make them differ more from each other in terms of gameplay experience so that the game feels richer. At the moment, we can change the image used, their movement, health, and action points, but that is it. I feel that we need more than that to flesh out the classes.

If we start to think about what primarily identifies such classes, at an initial and shallow glance, we'll probably arrive at the conclusion that their equipment and weapons are an integral part of how we expect those classes to be present in a game or story – dwarves with their shields, armors, and axes; elves so quick and shooting lots of arrows with their bows; wizards full of spells and wonder.

It is to support different classes, their equipment and gameplay, that we'll refactor many parts of our source code. Instead of going piece by piece and adding the feature we need for a given class when we're implementing that class, I think it is better to go ahead and add all the features first and then finish the chapter by creating each class section by section. That is actually more fun as well since all the features are in place, and you can simply be creative with your class creation.

Since there is a bit of tight coupling between some parts of our game, it is best that I explain what are the features we're adding to the game before going over the source code, as for some features to work, multiple changes need to be done across multiple files.

Support for defensive bonuses

Dwarves are famous for carrying shields; paladins are often in full armor. Being able to add support for equipment that helps with defending the player is something that we could have hacked by patching the `turn` and `refresh` function in every item to add values to the player health points, but that would be a hell to maintain and very hackish.

What we will do instead is make sure that all the items have a new function called protection that returns a number. Items that don't offer any protection should return zero. This way, to make a shield, we create an item and make it return a number larger than zero.

Then we patch the attack routines in the dungeon module to take this into account. The damage needs to be the attack value minus the protection offered by the equipped items from the victim.

Support for ranged attacks

Wizards and elves are famous for attacking from a distance. They are not usually very good when their enemies are too close, but from a distance, they are terrifying. Our current source code treats attacks as trying to move into a tile occupied by an enemy. We need to add support for ranged attacks for those classes to be able to be used in the game.

Adding such support requires many changes all around the place. First, we need to change the weapons to have a range value. Much like we're doing with `attack` and `protection`, we'll use a new function called `range`. Equipment that is supposed to be used only for melee combat will have a range of zero.

Now that we know the range of a given weapon, we need to have a way to input that we want to attack some specific tile with it. Right now, our player moves with the cursor keys or passes the turn with the spacebar, but there is no way to select a tile. To solve that, we're going to change the player character class to have a mouse input handler. We're just going to use it for ranged attacks. If the player has enough action points and clicks some tile with an enemy who is in range, then we'll make a ranged attack.

That requires changes to the dungeon module to support the ranged attacks. One crucial change is the animation; our current animation is the player tile going over to the enemy tile and back. We can't do that to ranged attacks; we need to animate some sort of projectile. We're going to do that by giving another tile, called an `attackTile`, to the weapons that are used for ranged attacks.

With those changes in place, we can finally begin to implement the classes. To start our refactor, let's patch the dungeon module to support those two features.

Refactoring the dungeon module

This initial sample combines the refactoring and the first class we're going to implement. The files are located in `chapter-6/example-1-warrior/`. One important alteration that was made to this sample is that the skeletons now walk three tiles per turn. This was done so that they'll become a challenge to some hero classes and just normal foes to others. If they kept walking just a single tile per turn, then a fast elf and a slow dwarf would face them the same way. With these changes, we alter the balance of peril in the dungeon. Talking about dungeons, let's continue the refactor by patching the dungeon module in `dungeon.js`.

We need to change `attackEntity` to support both bonuses and ranged attacks. First thing we'll do is change the function signature to contain an extra argument.

```
attackEntity: function (attacker, victim, rangedAttack = ↵
false) {
```

This `rangedAttack` argument is either in its default value, which is false, or a number that corresponds to the tile to be used for the ranged attack. This argument is also how the `attackEntity` will arbitrate between a melee and a ranged attack. We don't want that function to go poking into the player's equipped items to find the current weapon and then check the value returned by the range function of that item. That is too invasive and coupled; we'll delegate the responsibility of telling which kind of attack it is to the entity calling `attackEntity`. Be aware that this opens ranged attacks to monsters as well, which is fun.

```
attacker.moving = true
attacker.tweens = attacker.tweens || 0
attacker.tweens += 1

if (!rangedAttack) {
```

The function starts much like it already did, setting some tween counters for the attacker, and then it branches depending if it is a ranged attack or not.

```
this.scene.tweens.add({
    targets: attacker.sprite,
    onComplete: () => {
        attacker.sprite.x = this.map.tileToWorldX(attacker.x)
        attacker.sprite.y = this.map.tileToWorldX(attacker.y)
        attacker.moving = false
        attacker.tweens -= 1

        let attack = attacker.attack()
        let protection = victim.protection()
        let damage = attack - protection
```

```
        if (damage > 0) {
            victim.healthPoints -= damage

            this.log(`${attacker.name} does ${damage} ⏎
            damage to ${victim.name}.`)

            if (victim.healthPoints <= 0) {
                this.removeEntity(victim)
            }
        }
    },
    x: this.map.tileToWorldX(victim.x),
    y: this.map.tileToWorldY(victim.y),
    ease: "Power2",
    hold: 20,
    duration: 80,
    delay: attacker.tweens * 200,
    yoyo: true
})
} else {
```

The tween remains basically the same, but notice that we have a new variable called protection that holds how much defensive bonus the victim has, and that that value is deducted from the damage applied to the victim.

The ranged attack is basically the same; we're only changing the parameters of the tween. We don't need it to yo-yo back and forth; when you shoot an arrow, you don't expect it to come back (unless you're implementing a boomerang). The timing for the animation needs to be increased because we're talking about larger distances between the starting and ending coordinates. If we keep those values the same, the animation becomes too fast to be seen.

```javascript
const x = this.map.tileToWorldX(attacker.x)
const y = this.map.tileToWorldX(attacker.y)
const sprite = dungeon.scene.add.sprite(x, y, "tiles", ⏎
rangedAttack).setOrigin(0)

this.scene.tweens.add({
    targets: sprite,
    onComplete: () => {
        attacker.moving = false
        attacker.tweens -= 1

        let attack = attacker.attack()
        let protection = victim.protection()
        let damage = attack - protection
        if (damage > 0) {
            victim.healthPoints -= damage

            this.log(`${attacker.name} does ${damage} damage ⏎
            to ${victim.name}.`)

            if (victim.healthPoints <= 0) {
                this.removeEntity(victim)
            }
        }
        sprite.destroy()
    },
    x: this.map.tileToWorldX(victim.x),
    y: this.map.tileToWorldY(victim.y),
    ease: "Power2",
    hold: 20,
    duration: 180,
    delay: attacker.tweens * 200
})
```

The ranged attack uses a different tile than the player tile. That tile is used in a direct tween going from the player coordinates to the victim coordinates. To do that, we create a brand-new sprite, add it to the scene, and tween it. When the tween completes, we destroy that sprite as it is no longer useful. Besides that, all the rest of the code is the same as the melee one; we also take into account potential defensive bonuses there.

These changes assume that certain functions are present in all items; to make this real, we need to patch our generic item class.

Patching the generic item

The code for the generic item class is inside `items/genericItem.js`; we need to add two functions to it.

```
protection() {
    return 0
}
range() {
    return 0
}
```

Now we can be sure that the dungeon module will not barf when we use the items we already have built in an attack. With these code changes in place, the game should play exactly the same as it had in Chapter 5. The weapons will work the same, and since no item is offering any kind of protection or range, all the experience remains the same, which means it is time to change that.

To make it easier to implement multiple items, we created a generic item class and made all the items extend it, overriding what needed to change to make them unique. We'll take the same approach with the character classes. We'll create a basic hero class that feels pretty much like our current player character and then make the other class expand on it.

Creating a basic hero class

We'll create a classes folder to hold all the character classes and place basicHero.js there as our base class for all the future classes we'll implement. It is tricky that I'm calling this feature character classes, borrowing a concept from RPGs, and also implementing this as JS classes. It makes it a bit cumbersome to talk about two things that use the same word and are being implemented at the same time. So, we'll implement character classes using JavaScript classes.

Refactoring our previous player.js (that is gone from this sample) into the basicHero.js is also a good opportunity to change how some aspects of that class work.

I'm not happy with how we handle input events in it, and since we must also implement handling mouse input, we'll refactor input handling out of the turn function. We'll use that function for stuff that needs to happen every turn, but that is not related to player input. For example, if the player's health points are too low, we'll tint the player sprite red.

We're going to refactor that input handler; we have to toggle equipment into something that also handles movement. To do that is basically to copy and paste the code from turn into a new function to be called from that handler. A mouse input handler will also be added to handle ranged attacks. There is a need to be careful as both handlers are also active when it is not the player's turn, so they will need to double check if the player has action and movement points before they do anything.

Up to Chapter 5, when the player's movement point reached zero, the turn was over. That meant that we could end up with unspent action points. That was not a problem because attacking was tied to moving, so without movement points, the player couldn't attack and spend their action point.

Now, with the ranged attack option, we need to make sure that the player's action points are changed to zero when the turn is over or they will be able to shoot arrows out of their turn. The easiest way to do that would be to check if both movement and action points are zero before passing the turn. The problem with that approach is that sometimes the user has nothing to do with their action points and no way to spend them. That would force them to use the spacebar to pass the turn at every turn that they don't fully spend both point pools and lead to a lot of friction for gameplay.

To solve that, we'll keep passing the turn when the movement is over, but we'll make sure that when the player's movement points reach zero, their action points will also be reduced to zero at the moment. This way, the player can keep walking without spending their action points, and the game loop remains the same.

This leads to an important aspect of the gameplay of our *Nano Dungeon*; it is a "move last" kind of game where you need to attack and take action before spending all your movement points. This is a design decision, and your own game project might have a different way of working this out. It needed to be acknowledged though because this is part of how the game feels and will influence tactics, which should feedback into all of the game design.

So let's go ahead and implement the basic hero class.

```
import dungeon from "../dungeon.js"

export default class BasicHero {
    constructor(x, y) {
        this.name = "The Hero"
        this.movementPoints = 1
        this.actionPoints = 1
        this.healthPoints = 30
        this.x = x
        this.y = y
        this.tile = 29
```

```
    this.moving = false
    this.type = "character"
    this.items = []

    dungeon.scene.input.keyboard.on("keyup", (event) => {
        if (!this.over()) {
            this.processInput(event)
        }
    });

    dungeon.scene.input.on("pointerup", (event) => {
        if (!this.over()) {
            this.processTouchInput(event)
        }
    });
}
```

That code is quite familiar to us, except for the removal of the cursor property that handled the cursor keys and the addition of two event handlers, one for when a key is released and another for when a mouse button is released (or a finger is lifted from the screen).

Acting when the key, mouse, or finger is up is for a very specific reason. If you keep them down, the event repeats, and the frequency is very fast. Handling keydown and pointerdown would cause our handler to fire multiple times while the key or finger is down; that would make the game buggy. If you try replacing that keyup with keydown and try to have the player's character walk, you'll see that it is basically impossible to walk a single tile; the event will fire multiple times even for the quickest keypress.

In both functions, we use the result of over to figure out if it is the player's turn or not before trying to handle any potential input.

Let's implement the processInput first. This function receives as an argument an event object from the keyup event.

```
processInput(event) {
    let oldX = this.x
    let oldY = this.y
    let moved = false
    let newX = this.x
    let newY = this.y

    let key = event.key
```

So far so good, the code is quite similar to our previous code used inside the turn function. The main difference is that we're setting a key variable to hold the value of the key that was pressed.

```
    // Equip items
    if (!isNaN(Number(key))) {

        if (key == 0) {
            key = 10
        }

        this.toggleItem(key - 1)
    }
```

The first check is to see if the key was one of the number keys that toggle equipment.

```
    // Pass the turn
    if (event.keyCode == 32) {
        this.movementPoints = 0
        this.actionPoints = 0
    }
```

In this sample, we added a handler for the spacebar key. Pressing it causes the player to pass their turn. This is useful as a tactical resource for the player in such occasions like they want a monster to draw near or a potion to make effect, without changing their position on the map or even simply not using all their movement points.

```
// Movement decision
if (event.key == "ArrowLeft") {
    newX -= 1
    moved = true
}

if (event.key == "ArrowRight") {
    newX += 1
    moved = true
}

if (event.key == "ArrowUp") {
    newY -= 1
    moved = true
}

if (event.key == "ArrowDown") {
    newY += 1
    moved = true
}
```

Instead of using this.cursor as in the previous samples, we're now using the value of event.key to check if any cursor key was pressed. It is quite similar to the previous code, but since all that keyboard input handling logic is now contained in its own function, it becomes easier to maintain.

```
// Execute movement
if (moved) {
    this.movementPoints -= 1
```

```
if (!dungeon.isWalkableTile(newX, newY)) {
    let entity = dungeon.entityAtTile(newX, newY)

    // Check if entity at destination is an enemy
    if (entity && entity.type == "enemy" && this. ↵
    actionPoints > 0) {
        const currentWeapon = this.currentWeapon()
        const rangedAttack = currentWeapon.range() > ↵
        0 ? currentWeapon.attackTile || currentWeapon. ↵
        tile : false
        dungeon.attackEntity(this, entity, rangedAttack)
        this.actionPoints -= 1
        this.movementPoints += 1
    }
}
```

The combat handling code needed adjustments. The game has been coded in a way that the player can only equip one weapon at a time. If they equipped a ranged weapon, then attacking with it requires checking to see if the enemy is in range and passing the attack weapon's attackTile to the dungeon.attackEntity function (and thus making it a ranged attack). This means that even in close combat, the player with a ranged weapon will still use that to attack. It is up to the player to equip another weapon if the monsters are drawing near. Since equipping a weapon is a free action (it doesn't cost any action point), the player can switch weapons during their turn to best fit their situation.

```
// Check if entity at destination is an item
if (entity && entity.type == "item" && ↵
this.actionPoints > 0) {
    this.items.push(entity)
    dungeon.itemPicked(entity)
```

```
        dungeon.log(`${this.name} picked ${entity. ↵
        name}: ${entity.description}`)
        this.actionPoints -= 1
    } else {
        newX = oldX
        newY = oldY
    }

  }
```

Picking an item remains the same as previously. If there is an entity on the destination tile and it is an item, then the player picks it up and moves into its tile.

```
    if (newX !== oldX || newY !== oldY) {
        dungeon.moveEntityTo(this, newX, newY)
    }
  }
}
```

Lastly, it is just a matter of actually moving the player's character. Mouse and touch input are a bit different. Selecting a tile to be the target of a ranged attack is the only action we're doing with mouse input, so its handler is much simpler. It is very convenient that Phaser includes the input plugin[1] by default in a scene. It makes handling input much easier.

```
processTouchInput(event) {
    let x = dungeon.map.worldToTileX(event.worldX)
    let y = dungeon.map.worldToTileY(event.worldY)

    let entity = dungeon.entityAtTile(x, y)
```

---

[1]Input plugin documentation: https://photonstorm.github.io/phaser3-docs/
Phaser.Input.InputPlugin.html

The coordinates where the mouse or touch input happened are exposed in many ways in the event handler. The values are mapped to our world and camera settings when accessed using worldX and worldY and thus easily convertible to tile coordinates to use to obtain the potential entity at that location with the aid of the dungeon module.

```
if (entity && entity.type == "enemy" && this.
actionPoints > 0) {
    const currentWeapon = this.currentWeapon()
    const rangedAttack = currentWeapon.range() > 0 ? ↵
    currentWeapon.attackTile || currentWeapon.tile : false
    const distance = dungeon.distanceBetweenEntities ↵
    (this, entity)
    if (rangedAttack && distance <= currentWeapon. ↵
    range()) {
        dungeon.attackEntity(this, entity, rangedAttack) ↵
        this.actionPoints -= 1
    }
}
}
```

Executing a ranged attack requires the player to have action points available and clicking an enemy tile that is in range. If all those checks are OK, then the attack can proceed.

Without further changes, we'd introduce a very serious bug in our game: the player would be able to attack enemies when it is not their turn. If they ended their turn with leftover action points, and the enemies moved in range, they'd be able to click and attack them. To solve that, we must patch the over function to make sure that when we exhaust the movement points, we also set the action points to zero and pass the turn.

```
over() {
    let isOver = this.movementPoints <= 0 && !this.moving

    if (isOver && this.UIheader) {
        this.UIheader.setColor("#cfc6b8")
        this.actionPoints = 0
    } else {
        this.UIheader.setColor("#fff")
    }

    return isOver
}
```

Adding `this.actionPoints = 0` in the case that the turn is over will prevent that bug.

It is now time to implement our first character class, the warrior.

Creating a warrior class

If we're being honest, our basic hero class is kind of the warrior class; the changes will be basically cosmetic and in regard to movement. Also, we changed the basic hero constructor not to give the player any equipment and removed the initialization call to the dungeon module. All the character classes will use the constructor to customize the class and then call `dungeon.initializeEntity` on their own.

Next to `basicHero.js` is the file for the warrior class; it is called `warrior.js`. In it we'll customize the constructor to give the warrior more movement points and more action points than the basic hero. We'll also give it a basic sword. There is no need to customize the sprite tile because the basic hero sprite is the warrior sprite; that'll change the other classes though.

```
import BasicHero from "./basicHero.js"
import Sword from "../items/sword.js"
import dungeon from "../dungeon.js"
```

All character classes will import the basic hero class (so it can be extended), any items we want to give to the player at the start of the game, and the dungeon module (so it can initialize the entity at the end of the constructor).

```
export default class Warrior extends BasicHero {
    constructor(x, y) {
        super(x, y)

        this.name = "Warrior"
        this.movementPoints = 3
        this.actionPoints = 2

        this.items.push(new Sword())
        this.toggleItem(0)

        dungeon.initializeEntity(this)
    }
```

It is very good to benefit from the new class keyword in JS; extending the basic hero class removes the need to write a ton of repetitive boilerplate when creating new hero archetypes. Maintaining and improving code that is shared between all archetypes becomes much easier as well since it is all self-contained in the basic hero class.

```
    refresh() {
        this.movementPoints = 3
        this.actionPoints = 2
    }
}
```

While the basic hero would walk one tile and be able to attack only once per turn, the warrior can walk more and execute more attacks. Playing with that hero has a totally different feel than the previous basic hero we used. With extra movement and attacks, the player is not as fearful of being mobbed and can be more bold in their movement and tactics.

To make it easier to experiment with multiple character classes, we're going to create a `classes.js` file that is just a new object to hold reference to all the character classes. This file will be imported by the world scene, thus making all archetypes available there. Changing what hero we're using will be just a matter of changing what class is initialized in the world scene.

```
import Warrior from "./classes/warrior.js"

const classes = {
    Warrior
}

export default classes
```

Importing that file in the world scene is straightforward.

```
import classes from "./classes.js"
```

And so is initializing a warrior inside the `create` function in the world scene.

```
dungeon.player = new classes.Warrior(15, 15)
```

All the changes needed to further explore hero archetypes are in place, and our first class, the warrior, although very similar to our old basic hero, plays in a much bolder style. Let's implement another class now; it is time to create our first dwarf.

Creating a dwarf

Dwarves are a staple of the fantasy genre. They've evolved a lot in recent fiction beyond what we normally associate with the archetype, and it would be cool to see more games benefit from more flexible dwarves. Our sample will be quite old-school though and focus on the oldest features we associate with that archetype. Our dwarves will be protected, walk less than a warrior, and pack a strong melee attack.

From this section onward, each hero archetype will be contained in its own sample. The code for the dwarf is in chapter-6/example-2-dwarf/.

As mentioned earlier in the chapter, giving distinctive items to a class makes it feel more fleshed out and fun to play. For the dwarf, we're going to create a weapon suitable for a dwarf, then work on the class. The dwarf basic weapon will be an axe, and the code for it is in items/axe.js.

```
import GenericItem from "./genericItem.js"

import dungeon from "../dungeon.js"

export default class Axe extends GenericItem {
    constructor(x, y) {
        super(x,y)
        this.tile = 934
        this.name = "An Axe"
        this.description = "A basic axe. Causes between 2 ↵
        and 7 damage."
        this.weapon = true

        dungeon.initializeEntity(this)

    }
```

```
    damage() {
        return Phaser.Math.Between(2, 7)
    }
}
```

The item is implemented much like the sword we created in previous chapters but with a distinctive tile, description, and damage. Any prudent dwarf wouldn't walk into a dungeon without a shield. Let's create another item, this one inside items/shield.js.

```
import GenericItem from "./genericItem.js"
import dungeon from "../dungeon.js"

export default class Sword extends GenericItem {
    constructor(x, y) {
        super(x,y)
        this.tile = 776
        this.name = "A Shield"
        this.description = "A basic shield. Gives +1 ↵
        protection."

        dungeon.initializeEntity(this)
    }

    protection() {
        return 1
    }
}
```

The shield is a simple item. Besides metadata such as tile and description, all it does is add a defensive bonus to the player by returning a positive value from the protection function. Remember that cursed gem we created some time ago? You could have a cursed shield that returned

a negative number from protection and thus caused extra damage to the
player at every attack or a cursed hammer that did that but also inflicted
a ton of damage on enemies. So the player would be constantly torn
between using the strong weapon and also receiving extra damage, and
using something weaker but being better protected.

Implementing the dwarf is also easy; the code is in classes/dwarf.js.

```javascript
import dungeon from "../dungeon.js"
import BasicHero from "./basicHero.js"
import Axe from "../items/axe.js"
import Shield from "../items/shield.js"

export default class Dwarf extends BasicHero {
    constructor(x, y) {
        super(x, y)

        this.name = "Dwarf"
        this.movementPoints = 2
        this.actionPoints = 2
        this.healthPoints = 35
        this.tile = 61

        this.items.push(new Axe())
        this.toggleItem(0)

        this.items.push(new Shield())
        this.toggleItem(1)

        dungeon.initializeEntity(this)
    }

    refresh() {
        this.movementPoints = 2
        this.actionPoints = 2
    }
}
```

At the constructor, you can see that the dwarf moves less tiles than the warrior but has more health points. They are also equipped with both an axe and a shield, which will provide an extra layer of protection to the hero. Playing such character is different than playing the warrior. The warrior favors bold movement tactics and attacking multiple times; the dwarf is more like a tank, slow moving but relentless.

Don't forget to add the new class to `classes.js`.

```
import Warrior from "./classes/warrior.js"
import Dwarf from "./classes/dwarf.js"

const classes = {
    Warrior,
    Dwarf
}

export default classes
```

And change the world scene to use it.

```
dungeon.player = new classes.Dwarf(15, 15)
```

A more complex archetype to implement is the one we'll be seeing next, the cleric.

Creating a cleric

The cleric is a class that is constantly shifting in the fantasy genre. What people appear to agree with it is that the cleric is like a warrior that has access to healing powers through some holy or divine entity they're linked with. There is a spectrum of cleric-ness going on in the game and fantasy worlds, from warriors with healing powers to basically medieval fantasy medic monks that don't fight; there is a lot of room for interpretation and creative design.

Keeping our laser focus on building a simple game, our cleric will have one unique ability that other classes don't have. The cleric will heal a bit every turn. It is simple but quite effective. Every turn, the cleric will heal one health point during refresh. In a multiplayer game, the cleric would possess the ability to heal others, but in this game, there are no other hero characters, so healing themselves is good enough.

In many older TTRPG games, the cleric was prevented from using edged weapons. We can't really implement that in our dungeon, unless we start adding new properties to the generic item class to tell us what kind of weapon a given item is. Instead, we'll give the cleric a non-edged weapon upon its creation on the constructor and let the player decide if they want to switch it to an edged weapon as they play the game and collect loot.

The default weapon for the cleric will be a hammer; the code for the cleric sample is in chapter-6/example-3-cleric, and the hammer is in items/hammer.js.

```
import GenericItem from "./genericItem.js"
import dungeon from "../dungeon.js"

export default class Hammer extends GenericItem {
    constructor(x, y) {
        super(x,y)
        this.tile = 933
        this.name = "A warhammer"
        this.description = "A basic warhammer. Causes ↵
        between 3 and 8 damage."
        this.weapon = true

        dungeon.initializeEntity(this)

    }
```

```
    damage() {
        return Phaser.Math.Between(3, 8)
    }
}
```

It's the same kind of weapon template as the sword and the axe; it causes more damage though.

```
import dungeon from "../dungeon.js"
import BasicHero from "./basicHero.js"
import Hammer from "../items/hammer.js"

export default class Cleric extends BasicHero {
    constructor(x, y) {
        super(x, y)

        this.name = "Cleric"
        this.movementPoints = 3
        this.actionPoints = 2
        this.healthPoints = 40
        this.tile = 30

        this.items.push(new Hammer())
        this.toggleItem(0)

        dungeon.initializeEntity(this)
    }
```

As we can see there, the cleric walks and attacks like the warrior, but they have more health points, making them a bit better than warriors to play to be honest.

The healing action will happen inside the refresh function. If the health points of the player drop below 40 points, they start healing at a rate of one point per turn. If the player's health is too low, it pays to go to an isolated place in the dungeon and keep pressing the space bar to pass the turns and heal.

```
refresh() {
    this.movementPoints = 3
    this.actionPoints = 2

    // Clerics heal a bit every turn
    if (this.healthPoints < 40) {
        this.healthPoints += 1
        dungeon.log("Cleric heals 1 hp")
    }
  }
}
```

Clerics should play differently than a warrior. Even though they possess all the characteristics of the warrior class plus healing, playing a cleric is a game of moving forward and retreating for a bit to heal before moving more. The cleric class is better suited for more dangerous dungeons, but clearing the dungeon with the warrior with all its limitations is a challenge that many players will enjoy.

To try it out, you need to add it to the classes.js and switch which class is used in the world scene, just like we did with the dwarf.

Finally, we're about to implement a class with a ranged weapon; here comes the elf.

Creating an elf

Elves are such a versatile archetype that is a bit hard to pinpoint what would be their defining characteristic in terms of gameplay. Just like the previous archetypes mentioned, elves have seen an explosion in terms of different ways on how they are perceived in works of fantasy. What we'll focus on is a nimble character that shoots a lot of arrows.

They will be weaker than the other character classes we have; this way, the player will prioritize ranged combat and be quite wary of enemies drawing too close. Their default weapon will be a bow. Since this is just a sample, we're giving them infinite arrows, but if you want a better design, you could use an internal property on the item to count how many arrows the player has left.

The code for this sample is in chapter-6/example-4-elf/, and our new bow in items/bow.js.

```js
import GenericItem from "./genericItem.js"
import dungeon from "../dungeon.js"

export default class Bow extends GenericItem {
    constructor(x, y) {
        super(x,y)
        this.tile = 901
        this.attackTile = 872
        this.name = "A Bow"
        this.description = "A bow and arrows. Causes ↵
        between 1 and 3 damage. Range is four tiles."
        this.weapon = true

        dungeon.initializeEntity(this)

    }

    damage() {
        return Phaser.Math.Between(1, 3)
    }

    range() {
        return 5
    }
}
```

This is our first ranged weapon. Its range is five tiles; that counts the tiles the player is in and the tile the enemy is in. So by having a range of five, it means that you can fire at an enemy as long as there are up to three empty tiles between you both.

The elf class is in classes/elf.js.

```
import dungeon from "../dungeon.js"
import BasicHero from "./basicHero.js"
import Bow from "../items/bow.js"

export default class Elf extends BasicHero {
    constructor(x, y) {
        super(x, y)

        this.name = "Elf"
        this.movementPoints = 4
        this.actionPoints = 3
        this.healthPoints = 20
        this.tile = 56

        this.items.push(new Bow())
        this.toggleItem(0)

        dungeon.initializeEntity(this)
    }

    refresh() {
        this.movementPoints = 4
        this.actionPoints = 3
    }
}
```

Nimbler than the other classes, the elf can move four tiles per turn. This allows the player to move closer to the enemies, attack, and then move away, basically leading a sort of guerilla approach to dungeoneering. With three action points per turn, the elf can shoot three times per turn, allowing it to attack (and if lucky kill) multiple targets before they have a chance to move.

Our final character class for the chapter will be the wizard.

Creating a wizard

Wizards come in many kinds, so many that we have different names to refer to them – sorcerers, conjurers, and so on – but in our game, we're going back to basics. Inspired by RPGs, our wizard will be an old-school savvy hero who uses scrolls to memorize spells and cast them.

In essence, these scrolls will be ranged weapons. They will appear as scrolls in the player's user interface, and their attack tile will look like a spell, but internally they'll behave just like the bow from the elf. The code for the wizard is in chapter-6/example-5-wizard/.

We need to do just a bit of housekeeping before implementing our first scroll. In our spritesheet graphics, we don't have many images for scrolls. They are all the same color, and that would make it difficult for the player to figure out which one to equip as they'd look all the same. To solve this problem, we'll introduce sprite tinting to the game. This allows us to paint over a sprite with any color of our choosing. It requires us to patch the dungeon module and the basic hero.

Let's start with the basic hero patching. What we need to do is double check if the item being added to the interface has a tint property, and if it does, use that in the sprite. Inside the refreshUI function, we're changing the first if clause to be

```
if (!item.UIsprite) {
    let x = this.UIitems[i].x + 10
    let y = this.UIitems[i].y + 10
    item.UIsprite = this.UIscene.add.sprite(x, y, "tiles", ↵
    item.tile)
    if (item.tint) {
        item.UIsprite.tint = item.tint
        item.UIsprite.tintFill = true
    }
}
```

The interesting addition is the internal if clause that checks for a tint value and applies it.[2]

A similar change is needed in the initializeEntity function of the dungeon module so that tinted sprites appear with the same tint in the dungeon and in the player's user interface.

```
initializeEntity: function (entity) {
    if (entity.x && entity.y) {
        let x = this.map.tileToWorldX(entity.x)
        let y = this.map.tileToWorldY(entity.y)
        entity.sprite = this.scene.add.sprite(x, y, "tiles", ↵
        entity.tile)
        entity.sprite.setOrigin(0)
        if (entity.tint) {
            entity.sprite.tint = entity.tint
            entity.sprite.tintFill = true
        }
    }
},
```

---

[2]Sprite tint documentation: https://photonstorm.github.io/phaser3-docs/ Phaser.GameObjects.Sprite.html#tint__anchor

We should also tint the attack sprite used for ranged attacks. To do that, we'll patch the `attackEntity` function in the dungeon module. Since that function is not aware of what item is being used in the attack, we need to pass another argument to its call with the tint color to use. Like the ranged attack argument, this tint is optional and set to false by default.

```
attackEntity: function (attacker, victim, rangedAttack = ↵
false, tint = false) {
```

The optional tint is going to be used only for ranged attacks, so we add the following lines after the sprite creation for such attacks:

```
const sprite = dungeon.scene.add.sprite(x, y, "tiles", ↵
rangedAttack).setOrigin(0)

if (tint) {
    sprite.tint = tint
    sprite.tintFill = true
}
```

Having that argument declared there is not enough; we must use it from the attack handling routines of our basic hero class. So all the calls to `attackEntity` in both `processInput` and `processTouchInput` need to be patched to carry the tint.

```
processTouchInput(event) {
        let x = dungeon.map.worldToTileX(event.worldX)
        let y = dungeon.map.worldToTileY(event.worldY)

        let entity = dungeon.entityAtTile(x, y)

        if (entity && entity.type == "enemy" && this. ↵
        actionPoints > 0) {
            const currentWeapon = this.currentWeapon()
```

```
        const rangedAttack = currentWeapon.range() > 0 ? ↵
        currentWeapon.attackTile || currentWeapon.tile : ↵
        false
        const tint = currentWeapon.tint || false
        const distance = dungeon. ↵
        distanceBetweenEntities(this, entity)
        if (rangedAttack && distance <= currentWeapon. ↵
        range()) {
            dungeon.attackEntity(this, entity, ↵
            rangedAttack, tint)
            this.actionPoints -= 1
        }
    }
}
```

And in processInput, we used the exact same change, creating a tint constant and passing it to attackEntity.

These changes will open many opportunities for entity creation, especially once we start with procedural generation in the next chapters. Let's proceed to implement our first spell, the fireball, whose code is at items/scrolloffireball.js.

```
import GenericItem from "./genericItem.js"
import dungeon from "../dungeon.js"

export default class ScrollOfFireball extends GenericItem {
    constructor(x, y) {
        super(x,y)
        this.tile = 881
        this.tint = 0xdd0000
        this.attackTile = 335
        this.name = "A Scroll of Fireball"
```

```
        this.description = "A scroll of fireball. Causes ↵
        between 1 and 4 damage. Range is four tiles."
        this.weapon = true

        dungeon.initializeEntity(this)
    }
    damage() {
        return Phaser.Math.Between(1, 4)
    }
    range() {
        return 4
    }
}
```

The fireball is similar to the bow in its implementation; it is in essence
a simple ranged weapon. We added a red tint to it using the tint property
in the constructor so that it appears differently than the other spell scrolls
we're going to build. Fireballs are powerful, but their range is not that long.
A spell with a longer range is lightning, which is implemented in items/
scrolloflightning.js.

```
import GenericItem from "./genericItem.js"
import dungeon from "../dungeon.js"

export default class ScrollOfLightning extends GenericItem {
    constructor(x, y) {
        super(x,y)
        this.tile = 881
        this.tint = 0x0022ff
        this.attackTile = 413
        this.name = "A Scroll of Lightning"
```

```
        this.description = "A scroll of Lightning. Causes ↵
        between 1 and 2 damage. Range is seven tiles."
        this.weapon = true

        dungeon.initializeEntity(this)
    }

    damage() {
        return Phaser.Math.Between(1, 2)
    }

    range() {
        return 7
    }
}
```

The code is almost the same as the fireball, but it is a weaker spell with a longer range. The player controlling the wizard needs to switch them as the monsters draw near. Let's implement a final potion, a health potion, in items/healthPotion.js.

```
import GenericItem from "./genericItem.js"
import dungeon from "../dungeon.js"

export default class HealthPotion extends GenericItem {
    constructor(x,y) {
        super(x,y)
        this.tile = 761
        this.name = "Health Potion"
        this.description = "A potion that cures between 3 ↵
        and 5 health points when."

        dungeon.initializeEntity(this)

    }
```

```
    equip(itemNumber) {
        const points = Phaser.Math.Between(3, 5)
        dungeon.log(`A warm feeling is felt when drinking the ↵
        potion as it restores ${points} health points.`)
        dungeon.player.healthPoints += points
        dungeon.player.removeItem(itemNumber)
    }
}
```

We're going to give a couple of health potions to the wizard. Dungeons are dangerous places, and wizards should go in with all the equipment possible. Talking about wizards, let's implement classes/wizard.js.

```
import dungeon from "../dungeon.js"
import BasicHero from "./basicHero.js"
import ScrollOfFireball from "../items/scrolloffireball.js"
import ScrollOfLightning from "../items/scrolloflightning.js"
import HealthPotion from "../items/healthPotion.js"

export default class Wizard extends BasicHero {
    constructor(x, y) {
        super(x, y)

        this.name = "Wizard"
        this.movementPoints = 3
        this.actionPoints = 1
        this.healthPoints = 20
        this.tile = 88

        this.items.push(new ScrollOfFireball())
        this.items.push(new ScrollOfLightning())
        this.items.push(new HealthPotion())
```

```
        this.items.push(new HealthPotion())
        this.toggleItem(1)

        dungeon.initializeEntity(this)
    }
    refresh() {
        this.movementPoints = 3
        this.actionPoints = 1
    }
}
```

Wizards are weak beings, easy to kill if the monster can actually attack them. They don't have a lot of movement points so the player needs to be clever (and a bit lucky) with their moves. To improve the odds of the wizard surviving, we have given them two health potions. Equipping them should restore a bunch of health points, but like the holy potion, they are single-use items.

Adding the wizard to classes.js and changing the class that is initialized in the world scene will let you play with that class.

Exercises

Can you create more character classes? How would a cat be used as a hero? Maybe it can't attack, and all the play is based on avoidance and stealth, with the cat having nine lives before permadeath actually strikes them down. What about a magical cat? You can give some scrolls to the cat and make it quite dangerous. There is a cat tile on the spritesheet, just saying.

Summary

This completes all the basic archetypes we set out to create at the beginning of the chapter. To implement the character classes, we had to patch a bit of our game code, but we now have a very flexible framework to let our creativity roam wild while we create items, monsters, and heroes.

It is important to understand how each of the character archetypes builds upon both genericItem.js and basicHero.js, overriding their properties and functions to create fleshed out experiences of various heroes that play differently from one another.

So far, all we implemented has been basic gameplay features needed to use as a base to build our roguelike. At the moment, the game doesn't feel roguelike; we're missing the most important ingredient which is the always fresh gameplay you get when you add procedural generation to the game. In the next chapter, we'll start on that path by adding procedurally generated entities to our dungeon.

CHAPTER 7

Procedurally Generated Monsters and Items

Finally, we have arrived at one of the cornerstones of roguelikes: procedural generation is probably one of the first things that comes to the mind of a player when they think about the genre, probably alongside thinking about permadeath and maybe ASCII graphics. Before we dive deeper into the code, it's best if we explain a bit about what procedural generation is and what it is good for and most importantly what role it plays in the scope of this book.

Procedural generation is a deep topic, and we cannot do it justice with the two chapters we have devoted to it in this book. This book is an introduction to roguelike development, an initial blueprint for you to experiment with and get a taste for the genre from a development point of view. We cannot explore all the potential algorithms, libraries, and techniques that have been so cleverly used by the mainstays of the genre, but we can take you on a tour of how it works and implement some procedural techniques in our game while giving you pointers on where to find more information about the various topics we're exploring.

© Andre Alves Garzia 2020
A. A. Garzia, *Roguelike Development with JavaScript*,
https://doi.org/10.1007/978-1-4842-6059-3_7

On this chapter, we are going to limit procedural generation to just two types of entities – items and enemies – we will leave the dungeon generation to the next chapter. As an author, I have struggled for a long time about how to approach the topic for this chapter. I wanted it to be fresh for those who have already interacted with procedural generation before, as I am sure some of you already did, while keeping it approachable and understandable for the developers who are seeing this for the first time. My solution was to create a system that was based on a common concept that should be known for all the readers of this book: tags.

Introducing tags

Tags are a pervasive concept in our networked life. They permeate all corners of most of the social networks we interact with and are a very recognizable jargon to build upon. We can think of tags as labels that we attribute to collections of characteristics and behaviors. They encompass an aspect of whatever is being represented in an easy to understand and fast to communicate way. As an example, picture a car in your mind. If you saw a picture of this car with a tag *#electric*, you'd instantly realize you're looking at an electric vehicle.

Another good property of tags is that they are composable. You can apply many tags to the same thing and have it be the sum of all of them. That car that was mentioned earlier could also have the tags *#fourbyfour*, *#manualshift*, and *#red* applied to it, giving you much more context about the vehicle.

This is what we are going to do in this book, create a system of tags that can be applied to entities to define their behavior or augment their characteristics. By the end of the chapter, we will have tags such as *#cursed* and *#golden* that we can apply to a sword to make it an attractive but dangerous weapon.

Aren't you describing mixins?

Mixins are a common pattern used in object-oriented programming for composition and code reuse. It is usually the answer for when you have a car class and a flying class and want to make a flying car class by mixing both classes. This is not exactly what our tag system will do. It will compose between different collections of features, but it will not do it in the shallow way that mixins work. By shallow I mean that usually developers opt for using mixins when they want an object to be the sum of the methods and properties of two or more classes. Our tag system will be different and work as pipelines.

Tags as pipelines

If tags were implemented as mixins, then the entities they are attached to would be the sum of the methods and properties of each tag. This does not match the way our entity system works. Our game entities have a lifecycle of methods – turn, over, refresh, and so on – which is well defined; attaching more functions to them will not work.

What works is attaching multiple versions of the lifecycle methods and making the code behave so that executing a method executes a pipeline of versions of that method. This way, every time some method is called, that method will be called for the entity and for each tag that is attached to that entity. Suppose there is a *#cursed* tag that subtracts 1 `healthPoint` from the entity every turn. For that to work, the tag would implement a `turn` function much like our entities do, and when the `turn` function for the entity is called, then the `turn` functions for all the tags attached to that entity are also called.

Making good tags

Tags work best when they are flexible. It is very tempting to just decompose the behaviors we already have into discrete units and call it a day, but that would be selling tags short.

In my opinion, tags work best when they have different meanings depending on the context. A boat with a tag *#sinking* is a bad thing; a submarine with the same tag is business as usual. The idea is to make tags be an advantage or a disadvantage depending on how they are applied. A #burning entity can lose `healthPoints` at every turn, but a *#burning* sword will give an attack bonus to the player and add the *#burning* tag to entities it damages. The tag is the same, *#burning*, but how it works depends on whether it is applied to the player, enemies, or to an item.

It will not be possible to make all tags be flexible like that; some will just be discrete units of reusable boring characteristics, but the more flexible tags we have, the more interesting our game (and our creative process) becomes.

Tags and procedural generation

Procedural generation can be summarized as the act of making code that generates fresh content and behavior for every game. That's the tweet length definition and is incomplete. You can think of procedural generation as a factory that pumps new fresh content on demand. Some of that content will be recognizable, but the overall experience will be fresh.

Procedurally generating tags make them lose their appeal in the first place as they will not be the instantly recognizable labels we have grown to love and understand. What we will do is use procedural generation to select and apply tags to items and enemies, thus creating fresh content for our levels.

You've met our skeleton; they are the only enemy we've implemented so far. Now imagine that procedural generation applied *#royal* to it, making it Count Skeletah, then applied *#going-somewhere* which meant that Count Skeletah doesn't actually care for the player's position and is instead busy going to a different destination, and finally applied *#vegan* which causes Count Skeletah to never harm the player. Underneath it all, it is still a skeleton, but the tags made it fresh and memorable.

As you are probably realizing, implementing all this will require a major refactoring of our code.

Adding support for tags

There is more work needed for this chapter's sample than just adding the tags and the necessary plumbing around that feature. For tags to be effective, there need to be entities for them to be attached to. So, in this chapter, we are going to do an overhaul of our enemies and items, adding more variety and customizing the ones we already have.

Because of that, we will build just a single example in this chapter. After we add all the code that is necessary to support tags and add more enemies, the chapter will go over implementing all the tags.

The code for this chapter is in `chapter-7/example-1-tags/`.

Making entities taggable

Our entities all have similar shapes, but they inherit from different classes. All hero classes inherit from `BasicHero` and the items from `GenericItem`. In this initial step of our refactor, we're going to make a new class called `Taggable` and make both classes mentioned inherit from it, so each hero class will be an instance of `BasicHero` which is an instance of `Taggable`, and the same is true for the items but with `GenericItem` instead of `BasicHero` of course.

Before diving into the code of the `Taggable` class, it might be better to explain how it will work. The main driving force is to minimize changes to the existing entities. Even though we'll end up touching most of the entities, it won't be because they need changes to support tags but because we need to tweak something there so that tags make sense with them and the experience of developing the game is more enjoyable.

Tags will be JavaScript objects, not classes, because we want the functions attached to them to be in the objects themselves and not their prototypes. When a tag is applied to an entity, its functions will be copied over to some special properties in the entity, and the entity's original function of the same name will be wrapped into a function that calls the original code plus all the functions that were inserted into that special property, like a pipeline.

Instead of making the tag system into a library, we're making the Taggable class so that it becomes easier to work with the entities themselves by leveraging this reference inside each tag code.

The code for the Taggable class is inside the taggable.js file. There will also be another file called tags.js, which we will create after this one to hold a reference to each available tag. The declaration for the new class and the import for the tags object are straightforward.

```
import tags from "./tags.js"

export default class Taggable {

}
```

Each function that is going to be implemented in this class should go inside that block defined by the class keyword. I am breaking them all into discrete functions here so that I can explain them, but in the code, they are all inside the class. Let us begin by the most important function, addTag, which is the one that will be called to attach a tag to an entity. To be able to fully grasp what that function is doing, let me first show you a simple tag. It will be easier to explain addTag if you have seen a tag before. The tag I am going to show is *#iron*.

```
const iron = {
    name: "Iron",
    initialize: function () {
        this.name = `Iron ${this.name}`
        this.tint = 0xccbc00
```

```
    if (this.sprite) {
        this.sprite.tint = this.tint
        this.sprite.tintFill = true
    }
},

attack(acc = 0) {
    if (acc > 0) {
        acc += 1
    }
    return acc
},

protection(acc = 0) {
    if (acc > 0) {
        acc += 1
    }
    return acc
}
}

export default iron
```

A tag is an object. It contains a name that describes it; an initialize function that is called when it is added to an entity, much like a constructor in a class; and one or more functions with the same name as the lifecycle functions our entities have.

Each of these functions that are shared between the tags and the entities always receives a first argument that is the resulting value from passing the function through the pipeline. In this iron tag sample, there is an attack function. This function will be called if the tag is applied to a weapon when the weapon is used to attack another entity. First, the entity's own attack function is going to be called; the resulting value will then be passed to the first attack function in the pipeline of tags. Each function in this pipeline will receive the returned value from the previous function called. This way, they all have an opportunity to alter that value before it is returned to whoever called it in the first place.

These functions need to be made with care because tags can be attached to different entities and thus end up affecting them in undesirable ways if you are not attentive to how the game works. For example, we know that any item returning a positive number from the protection function will be counted as defensive bonus when an entity is attacked. If you do not take that into account when creating a protection function for a tag, you might make your tag offer protective bonus for items that were not actually contributing to protection in the first place. That might be what you want, or might not; in any case, it is better to see if the previous value was a number and not change it if it was zero. This way attaching the iron tag to a sword will not add to the player's defensive bonus, but attaching it to a shield will.

This iron tag adds +1 to an attack value if applied to a weapon and +1 to a defensive bonus if applied to another item, and it has no effect whatsoever if applied to the player or the enemies since they don't make use of attack or protection functions.

It will become clearer as we go over the code together. Don't worry if you don't understand everything about that iron tag now; I've placed it there so that you have a real tag to refer to while reading the code for the addTag function.

```
addTag(template) {
    let tag = {}
    Object.assign(tag, template)

    let name = tag.name
    delete tag.name

    tag.initialize.apply(this)
    delete tag.initialize
```

```
let keys = Object.keys(tag)
keys.forEach(handlerName => {
    this.wrapFunction(handlerName)
    this.addTagHandler(handlerName, tag[handlerName])

})

if (!this._tags) {
    this._tags = [name]
} else {
    this._tags.push(name)
}

return this
}
```

The addTag function receives a template object as its argument; that object is a tag blueprint like the iron tag mentioned earlier. The first step in that function is to create a new object and copy the blueprint over. That is done so that each applied tag has its own object; if that was not the case, then applying the same tag to two or more different entities would end up all pointing to the same object, and that might lead to some quite complex debugging sessions.

As mentioned before, we are going to copy functions from the tag into the entity. But we are not going to copy all of them. The name is a property, and we will use it to reference the tag in other parts of the code, so we save a variable with it and remove it from the tag object. The initialize function is called once and then deleted from the object. If it was copied over, then when applying a second tag to an object, you would end up calling the initialize function from the first tag again. This has happened to me while developing this example; it took me a while to understand what was happening. What saved me was that during the execution of the

181

initialize function, I took care to rename the entity, so multiple calls to the same initialize function caused the final name of the entity to be *iron iron iron sword*, thus pointing me to where the problem was.

Returning this at the end of the addTag handler ensures that we can pass the resulting value into the functions that expect an entity such as the addEntity function of the turn manager module. Calling addTag on an entity results into having another entity.

Remember that since the code is using apply, the references to this are pointing at the entity the tag is being applied to and not to the tag itself. After initializing the tag, it is time to copy the functions over, making sure we wrap them into a pipeline. For each function in the tag, we add it to a tag handler attached to the entity with the addTagHandler function. Tag handlers are objects in which the key is the function name and the value is an array of functions. So in our sample iron tag, we have an attack function; that means that in the tag handler object, there will be a property called attack that will hold an array which will contain that attack function from the tag.

If we were simply populating that tag handler object, then calling a lifecycle method such as attack on the entity wouldn't cause the pipeline to run; to do that, we need to replace the entity function of the same name with a wrapper that calls itself and the pipeline; that is what the wrapFunction function will do.

After the copying is done, we add the tag name to an array of applied tags for the entity. This is done so that we can later inspect and figure out which tags were applied since the copying and manipulation of the properties of the entity don't leave a paper trail of where the new functions came from.

```
addTagHandler( handlerName , handler) {
    if (!this._tagHandlers) {
        this._tagHandlers = {}
    }
```

```
if (!this._tagHandlers[handlerName]) {
    this._tagHandlers[handlerName] = []
}

this._tagHandlers[handlerName].push(handler)
}
```

The addTagHandler function is a bit bureaucratic but easy to understand. The first two if clauses are just checking to see if there is a tag handler object attached to the entity and initializing it with a property for the function being overwritten if it is not present. In the case of the attack function for the iron tag, after executing the addTagHandler, the entity would be like

```
Entity = {
  _tagHandlers: {
    Attack: [function() … ]
  }
}
```

The secret sauce for the tag system is in the wrapFunction function.

```
wrapFunction(handlerName) {
    if (!this._tagHandlers || !this._tagHandlers ↵
    [handlerName]) {
        let originalFunction = this[handlerName]
        this[handlerName] = (...args) => {
            let ret = originalFunction.apply(this, args)
            return this.executeTag(handlerName, ret, ↵
            ...args)
        }
    }
}
```

Saving a reference to the original function in a closure allows us to overwrite the property value with a new function that when executed calls the original function and then also execute every single function in the tag handlers for that named function with the executeTag function.

If a *dagger* entity had an original attack function like

```
attack() {
  return 1
}
```

then after calling wrapFunction on attack, the new attack function would be like this pseudo code:

```
attack() {
  let originalFunction = <original attack function>
  let ret = originalFunction.apply(this, args)
    return this.executeTag(name, ret, ...args)
}
```

It is important to understand how wrapFunction works, how it captures the value of a function in a closure before overwriting the value of the property that originally pointed to it with a new function. That is what allows us to apply tags to unchanged entities and have it all work; we are overwriting their properties while holding references to the original code.

```
executeTag(handlerName, ret, ...args) {
    if (this._tagHandlers && this._tagHandlers [handlerName]) {
        this._tagHandlers[handlerName].forEach(handler => {
            args = [ret, ...args]
```

```
        ret = handler.apply(this, args)
    })
  }
  return ret
}
```

Executing a pipeline is a matter of iterating over the function that is present in an array while passing the resulting value of a preceding function into the next function, until all is done, and the final value is returned. If that code looks a bit difficult to understand, it might be because of its usage of the spread syntax[1] and of the apply method[2] which allows us to call functions while explicitly setting the value of this to match the entity.

Adding multiple tags to an entity would, at this point, necessitate that we chain calls to addTag like entity.addTag(iron).addTag(rusty); that kind of code is hard to generate with procedural generation. It is better that we have a function that accepts an array of tag names and then proceeds to add each of them to an entity. For that to work, there needs to be an object that holds references to each available tag; that is what the tags module will do. We are only going to create that module in the end, but we can use it now knowing that it has the references to the tags in an object where each property is the same name as a tag, like

```
tags = {
  iron: iron,
  rusty: rusty
}
```

[1]Spread syntax documentation: https://developer.mozilla.org/en-US/docs/Web/JavaScript/Reference/Operators/Spread_syntax
[2]Apply method documentation: https://developer.mozilla.org/en-US/docs/Web/JavaScript/Reference/Global_Objects/Function/apply

With such module available, we can implement addTags in terms of a loop around addTag.

```
addTags(templateNames) {

    templateNames.forEach(t => {
        if (tags[t]) {
            this.addTag(tags[t])
        }
    })
    return this
}
```

Always make sure that we return the entity, so that calls to addTag and addTags can be chained together and passed over to other modules.

Having a way to add a tag is just half of the game; we need to have a way to remove it as well. Imagine that a poison tag is applied to the player, and then after drinking a health potion, the poison is removed. There must be a way to go into the tag handlers and remove the functions that came from the poison tag. This is trickier than it seems at first glance because we are creating a new object every time we add a tag to an entity. That means that holding a tag in an object, and having an entity that had that tag applied, does not mean that the tag handlers in the entity are pointing at the functions in the tag object. They were copied into a new tag object in the addTag handler, and from that brand-new object, they were placed in the tag handlers from the entity. Reconciling that information is tricky because of the way Boolean operators work in JavaScript. Comparing two functions using == or === will only return true if they are actually pointing at the same function, not if they are copies of the same function.

To solve that, we are going to use the toString[3] method of functions that serializes a function back into a string, basically back into the source code, and then compare if they are the same. Since there is no change between the function held in the tag object and the ones in tag handlers, they should generate the same string and thus be able to be compared to one another once in string form.

We need to be able to do this comparison so that we can find inside the tag handlers which functions belong to each tag and remove them.

```
removeTag(template) {
    let tag = {}
    Object.assign(tag, template)

    let name = tag.name
    delete tag.name
    delete tag.initialize

    let keys = Object.keys(tag)
    keys.forEach(handlerName => {
        let functionAsString = tag[handlerName].toString()
        let handlersAsString = this._tagHandlers ↵
        [handlerName].map(handler => handler.toString())
        let index = handlersAsString.findIndex(handlerAsString
        => handlerAsString == functionAsString) ↵
        this._tagHandlers[handlerName].splice(index, 1)
    })

    let tagPosition = this._tags.findIndex(tag => tag == name)
    this._tags.splice(tagPosition, 1)
}
```

---

[3]Documentation for the toString method for functions: https://developer. mozilla.org/en-US/docs/Web/JavaScript/Reference/Global_Objects/ Function/toString

Removing a tag is a matter of going over all the properties of a tag object, checking to see if there is a matching function in the tag handlers for that entity and, if there is, removing that from the array, and removing the tag name from the list of applied tags.

Our Taggable class is now ready to be used. The easiest class to refactor and add support for being taggable is the basic hero class.

Making heroes taggable

There needs to be a remarkably simple alteration to the Basic Hero class to make it support tags. In the classes/basicHero.js, we need to change the imports at the top and the class declaration to

```
import dungeon from "../dungeon.js"
import Taggable from "../taggable.js"

export default class BasicHero extends Taggable {
    constructor(x, y) {
        super(x,y)
```

The rest remains basically the same. All that is needed is to import the Taggable class and make sure that the BasicHero is inheriting from it and make sure we call the superclass constructor.

Now, we can apply tags to heroes! Let us add support for doing the same on items.

Making items taggable

It is almost a copy and paste of the changes done to the basic hero class. Import the Taggable class, make sure GenericItem inherits from it, and remember to call its constructor. While keeping the rest of the class without any alteration. Even though the exact same changes are needed to support taggable enemies, in that specific case, we need to do more work.

```
import Taggable from "../taggable.js"

export default class GenericItem extends Taggable{
    constructor(x,y) {
        super(x, y)
```

Making enemies

Up until now, we had a single enemy entity, the skeleton, and that is not sufficient anymore. Like it was done with items and heroes, we are going to create a basic enemy class and make all enemies inherit from it. This basic class will contain generic behavior and stub functions, like how the generic item class is implemented. After implementing that, we are going to rework the skeleton to be built on top of the new class and then add some more enemy classes.

All enemy classes will be placed inside an enemies/ folder that exists next to classes/ and items/.

A basic enemy class

Usually, a roguelike has more variation of enemies than it does of available hero archetypes. Of course, there are roguelikes that use procedural generation to generate both of them and thus have basically infinite combinations, but that is not the case I am making here; what I want to focus is that if we design the basic enemy class well, it becomes easier to create and maintain various monsters, easier than maintaining different hero classes.

For the purposes of our sample game, all monsters work the same. They are placed in the dungeon and walk around. Sometimes, if the conditions are right, they attack the player. When they die, they might drop some loot.

To implement the hero archetypes, we relied a lot on functions; almost everything is a class method, and we seldom use properties. That was done so that we could have more variation regarding what happens when a method is called. In the monster's case, we will do different. In the basic enemy constructor, we will set a lot of instance properties. The lifecycle methods such as over and refresh will work in a generic manner, but considering such properties, this way enemy variation is more about altering those values than crafting new functions. This means that tags that act on enemies will do most of their work in the initialize function so that they alter the enemy stats.

In the source for the basic enemy class, I will make use of some functions that we have not created yet. I will explain what they do, and later in the chapter, they will be created.

A lot of work will be done in this basic class; then the monsters will become easier to create afterward.

The source for this class is in enemies/basicEnemy.js.

```
import dungeon from "../dungeon.js"
import tm from "../turnManager.js"
import Taggable from "../taggable.js"
import { getRandomItem } from "../items.js"
import GenericItem from "../items/genericItem.js"
```

The basic enemy class needs access to the dungeon module to be able to display text information on the UI. The turn manager is used to be able to add loot to the dungeon when the enemy is killed. As with the other entity types, basic enemy will inherit from the Taggable class. The last two imports are from things we have not implemented yet. Like tags.js will be a module that holds references to all the available tags, the items.js will be a module with references and auxiliary functions for dealing with the available items. Access to those functions is needed to be able to figure out which item to drop when the enemy is killed. As for the generic item import, I will explain that in just a second.

```
export default class BasicEnemy extends Taggable {
    constructor(x, y) {
        super(x, y)
        this.name = "Basic Enemy"
        this.movementPoints = 1
        this.actionPoints = 1
        this.healthPoints = 1
        this.maxHealthPoints = this.healthPoints
        this.moving = false
        this.weapon = new GenericItem()
```

Like our previous entities, the basic entity extends the Taggable class and initializes some properties that all entities need. A surprising line is the last one in this snippet of source code; we're creating a weapon property with a dummy item. That is because later in the chapter, there will be alterations to the dungeon module attackEntity function. In the previous chapter, that function signature was

```
attackEntity: function (attacker, victim, rangedAttack = ↵
false, tint = false) {
```

That meant that it was up to the entity to figure out the values for rangedAttack and tint. In this chapter, that signature will be altered to something that is easier to maintain and more flexible:

```
attackEntity: function (attacker, victim, weapon) {
```

The intention behind changing that is to help with weapons containing tags, but that will be better explained in the section about the dungeon module refactor. For now, it suffices to say that since to call the attackEntity, the entity must pass a weapon as an argument, and that is why a dummy weapon item is created.

```
this.refreshRates = {
    movementPoints: 1,
    actionPoints: 1,
    healthPoints: 0
}
```

Instead of hardcoding values in the refresh function, we're adding values to the constructor which can be manipulated by tags during their initialize call. These values will be used by the basic enemy implementation of refresh.

```
this.damage = {
    max: 4,
    min: 1
}

this.defense = {
    max: 0,
    min: 0
}
```

Both attack and protection will use values set by the constructor. This will enable us to create new monsters by simply creating new classes and just implementing a new constructor or to radically alter a monster by applying a tag.

```
this.loot = []
this.x = x
this.y = y
this.tile = 26
this.type = "enemy"
```
}

The final lines of the constructor are known to us; they just set the final properties needed by the enemy.

```
refresh() {
    this.movementPoints = this.refreshRates.movementPoints
    this.actionPoints = this.refreshRates.actionPoints
    if (this.refreshRates.healthPoints > 0 && ↵
    this.healthPoints <= this.maxHealthPoints) {
        this.healthPoints += this.refreshRates.healthPoints
    }
}
```

Because we set all those properties in the constructor, the refresh function becomes a generic function that just works for all enemies. The presence of this.maxHealthPoints and this.refreshRates. healthPoints allows for the creation of monsters that heal some healthPoints at every turn. Setting that refresh rate to zero on the basic monster makes sure that we don't start healing all the monsters we create.

```
attack() {
    return Phaser.Math.Between(this.damage.min, ↵
    this.damage.max)
}

protection() {
    return Phaser.Math.Between(this.defense.min, ↵
    this.defense.max)

}
```

Generic implementations of attack and protection based on minimum and maximum values set on the constructor are enough for all our monsters. Remember that the idea behind these is to be able to alter the value returned by these functions with tags as the tags pipeline is processed after these functions are called and passed the resulting values from them into the pipeline.

```
turn() {

}
```

Did I surprise you there? Turn is left blank because it will be determined by tags. Imagine that we have tags which contain the turn logic; one tag could make the monster chase the player regardless of where they are in the dungeon. That is how the skeleton behaved. That tag could be called #hunter. Another tag can make the enemy choose a place to go and just move there; that tag could be called #going-somewhere. Both these tags determine how the enemy will behave each turn; more specifically, they will execute the entity movement and attack. If the entity has a turn implementation that moves it, and a tag also has a move implementation, which move is the successful one? How will the movementPoints accounting work between multiple calls to turn?

To solve all these cases, we will group some tags into *monster behavior tags* and make sure that each enemy has one and only one of those tags attached to it. How the monster will behave on the dungeon will depend on that tag.

```
over() {
    let isOver = this.movementPoints == 0 && ↵
    this.actionPoints  == 0 && !this.moving

    if (isOver && this.UItext) {
        this.UItext.setColor("#cfc6b8")
    } else {
        this.UItext.setColor("#fff")
    }

    return isOver
}
```

Nothing to see in the over function; it is the exact same function we used for the skeleton in all the previous samples.

The next function is a bit different. It is the onDestroy function that is called when the monster is killed, and it is ready to drop some loot. In that function, we will make use of the yet to be implemented getRandomItem function. This function will return a random item with tags applied to it. The first two arguments are the coordinates for the item; the last two are how many tags to apply from the *modifier tag set* and the *effects tag set*; these sets are just arrays with tag names that fall into some common characteristics. The modifier set changes some characteristics of the item. The effects set causes some effect each turn.

Keeping track of entities and tags is a bit hard; that is why changes were made to the createUI function. Each enemy has a UI displayed on the user interface sidebar. The new createUI function will mark the sprite and text used by each enemy user interface as clickable. Clicking them will output a description of the entity into the text output on the sidebar. A new function is provided by the dungeon module called describeEntity that receives an entity and outputs its name, tags, and description.

```
createUI(config) {
    let scene = config.scene
    let x = config.x
    let y = config.y

    this.UIsprite = scene.add.sprite(x, y, "tiles", this.tile)
        .setOrigin(0)
        .setInteractive({ useHandCursor: true })

    if (this.tint) {
        this.UIsprite.tint = this.tint
    }

    this.UIsprite.on("pointerup", pointer => {
        if (pointer.leftButtonReleased()) {
            dungeon.describeEntity(this)
        }
    })
    this.UItext = scene.add.text(x + 20, y, this.name, { ↵
    font: '12px Arial', fill: '#cfc6b8' })
        .setInteractive({ useHandCursor: true })
    this.UItext.on("pointerup", pointer => {
        if (pointer.leftButtonReleased()) {
            dungeon.describeEntity(this)
        }
    })

    return 30
}
```

That is done by using `setInteractive` on the text and sprite. The `useHandCursor` makes the mouse pointer change to a hand when it is over those game elements, thus helping the player discover that they are clickable.

A handler `on("pointerup", ...)` is used to create a callback that calls `dungeon.describeEntity`. The same change was made in the basic hero class so that clicking items on the player's inventory displays their description as well.

The basic enemy class is ready; we're ready to rework our skeleton.

Revisiting the skeleton

The code for the new skeleton entity will be inside `enemies/skeleton.js`; it is very simple since most of the work is actually done by the basic enemy class.

```
import dungeon from "../dungeon.js"
import BasicEnemy from "./basicEnemy.js"

export default class Skeleton extends BasicEnemy {
    constructor(x, y) {
        super(x, y)
        this.name = `Skeleton`
        this.movementPoints = 3
        this.actionPoints = 1
        this.healthPoints = 4
        this.refreshRates = {
            movementPoints: 3,
            actionPoints: 1,
            healthPoints: 0
        }
```

```
this.damage = {
    max: 4,
    min: 1
}

this.x = x
this.y = y
this.tile = 26
this.type = "enemy"
this.weapon.name = "pike"

dungeon.initializeEntity(this)
    }
}
```

The whole skeleton is just a customization of the properties set by the basic enemy constructor. A weapon name is set because the new attackEntity will display it in the sidebar when an attack happens.

Creating a bat

The code for the bat is in enemies/bat.js; it is just a custom constructor as well.

```
import dungeon from "../dungeon.js"
import BasicEnemy from "./basicEnemy.js"

export default class Bat extends BasicEnemy {
    constructor(x, y) {
        super(x, y)
        this.name = `Bat`
        this.movementPoints = 5
        this.actionPoints = 1
```

```
this.healthPoints = 2
this.refreshRates = {
    movementPoints: 5,
    actionPoints: 1,
    healthPoints: 0
}

this.damage = {
    max: 3,
    min: 1
}

this.x = x
this.y = y
this.tile = 282
this.type = "enemy"
this.weapon.name = "bite"

dungeon.initializeEntity(this)
    }
}
```

The bat is weak both in terms of healthPoints and damage it can do, but it moves quite a lot, and depending on the tag applied to it, it will get close to the player pretty fast.

Making an orc

The orc source is at enemies/orc.js.

```
import dungeon from "../dungeon.js"
import BasicEnemy from "./basicEnemy.js"

export default class Orc extends BasicEnemy {
```

```
constructor(x, y) {
    super(x, y)
    this.name = `Orc`
    this.movementPoints = 2
    this.actionPoints = 1
    this.healthPoints = 4
    this.refreshRates = {
        movementPoints: 2,
        actionPoints: 1,
        healthPoints: 0
    }

    this.damage = {
        max: 5,
        min: 2
    }

    this.x = x
    this.y = y
    this.tile = 57
    this.type = "enemy"
    this.weapon.name = "club"

    dungeon.initializeEntity(this)
    }

}
```

The orc is slower than the bat and skeleton, but it packs a punch. Depending on which tag ends up being applied to them, they can get pretty powerful.

Making a troll

It might be obvious by now but the code for the troll is at enemies/troll.js.

```js
import dungeon from "../dungeon.js"
import BasicEnemy from "./basicEnemy.js"

export default class Troll extends BasicEnemy {
    constructor(x, y) {
        super(x, y)
        this.name = `Troll`
        this.movementPoints = 2
        this.actionPoints = 1
        this.healthPoints = 8
        this.refreshRates = {
            movementPoints: 2,
            actionPoints: 1,
            healthPoints: 0
        }

        this.damage = {
            max: 6,
            min: 3
        }

        this.x = x
        this.y = y
        this.tile = 286
        this.type = "enemy"
        this.weapon.name = "club"

        dungeon.initializeEntity(this)
    }

}
```

Trolls are the strongest enemy we implemented. They are harder to kill and cause a lot of damage.

With the enemies in place, we are ready to create an enemies module holding reference to all of them. This way we don't need to import individual enemy files in the source when we need them; we can just import this module. In this module, we'll also implement functions to get a random monster.

Implementing the enemies module

The enemies module is in the root folder for the sample, named enemies.js; this is a convention for all the entity modules. The hero classes are in the classes/ folder, but the module is in classes.js at the top level. The items and the enemies modules will all live in the top folder.

```
import Skeleton from "./enemies/skeleton.js"
import Orc from "./enemies/orc.js"
import Bat from "./enemies/bat.js"
import Troll from "./enemies/troll.js"
import { getRandomTagsForEnemy } from "./tags.js"

const enemies = {
    Skeleton,
    Orc,
    Bat,
    Troll
}

export default enemies

export function getRandomEnemy(x, y, modifierCount = 1, ↵
effectCount = 1) {
    let key = Phaser.Utils.Array.GetRandom(Object.keys(enemies))
```

```
    let tags = getRandomTagsForEnemy(modifierCount, effectCount)
    return new enemies[key](x, y).addTags(tags)
}
```

The module imports all the enemies we created and sets a default export that is an object holding references to them. The interesting part of the module is the getRandomEnemy function though that picks a random element from that object and applies random tags to it before returning. Once we implement the tags module, that function will become clearer, but I can forward to you that it is basically the same as this one; there are objects holding all the keys, and we pull tags from it and return them as an array of names to be used with addTags from the Taggable class.

I know that it is tricky to describe and understand how these heavily interlocked modules work with one another by seeing each one at a time. Seeing the source code in an editor makes it much easier as you can jump from one file to another more easily than in a book. By talking about the tags module in the final sections of this chapter, I can make sure you know how they are supposed to work by the time we reach the conversation about their implementation. Also, by leaving the tag creation to the end of the chapter, I hope to entice you to create more tags during the exercise section since it will all be fresh in your memory.

Creating the items module

Just like we implemented the enemies module, we must create an items module. Their shape is the same: a default export that is an object containing all the items and a named export that allows you to fetch a random item.

```
import Axe from "./items/axe.js"
import Bow from "./items/bow.js"
```

```javascript
import CursedGem from "./items/cursedGem.js"
import Gem from "./items/gem.js"
import Hammer from "./items/hammer.js"
import HealthPotion from "./items/healthPotion.js"
import LongSword from "./items/longSword.js"
import Potion from "./items/potion.js"
import ScrollOfFireball from "./items/scrolloffireball.js"
import ScrollOfLightning from "./items/scrolloflightning.js"
import Shield from "./items/shield.js"
import Sword from "./items/sword.js"
import { getRandomTagsForItem } from "./tags.js"

const items = {
    Axe,
    Bow,
    CursedGem,
    Gem,
    Hammer,
    HealthPotion,
    LongSword,
    Potion,
    ScrollOfFireball,
    ScrollOfLightning,
    Shield,
    Sword
}
```

```
export default items

export function getRandomItem(x, y, modifierCount = 1, ↵
effectCount = 1) {
    let key = Phaser.Utils.Array.GetRandom(Object.keys(items))
    let tags = getRandomTagsForItem(modifierCount, effectCount)
    return new items[key](x, y).addTags(tags)
}
```

The source for this module is in items.js. Unlike the enemies, there were no alterations to the items themselves in this chapter, so all that is needed was the creation of this module.

Refactoring the dungeon module

Some changes are needed in the dungeon module to better support tags and make our life easier. The enemy user interface displayed in the sidebar is clickable now, and so are the items on the player's inventory. Both call describeEntity that needs to be implemented.

```
describeEntity: function (entity) {
    if (entity) {
        let name = entity.name
        let description = entity.description || ""
        let tags = entity._tags ? entity._tags.map(t => ↵
        `#${t}`).join(", ") : ""

        dungeon.log(`${name}\n${tags}\n${description}`)
    }
}
```

Assembling a nice string and displaying it in the user interface are all that this function needs to do; in Figure 7-1, you can see how it looks when the sample is running.

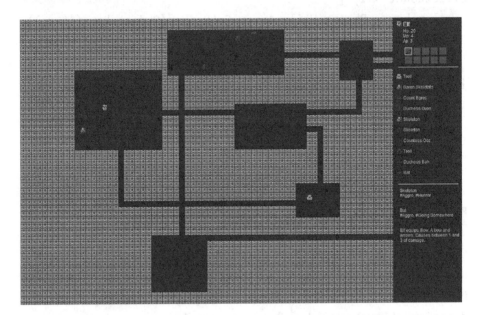

Figure 7-1. *Enemy descriptions*

Since in this chapter we're going to start positioning enemies in random places in the dungeon, we need a function to find ourselves a random walkable tile.

```
randomWalkableTile: function () {
    let x = Phaser.Math.Between(0, dungeon.level[0].length - 1)
    let y = Phaser.Math.Between(0, dungeon.level.length - 1)
    let tileAtDestination = dungeon.map.getTileAt(x, y)
    while (typeof tileAtDestination == "undefined" || ↩
    tileAtDestination.index == dungeon.sprites.wall) {
        x = Phaser.Math.Between(0, dungeon.level[0].length - 1)
```

```
      y = Phaser.Math.Between(0, dungeon.level.length - 1)
      tileAtDestination = dungeon.map.getTileAt(x, y)
   }
   return { x, y }
}
```

The function works by picking a random location and then checking if it is a wall or not; if it is, then it loops picking a different location. The resulting value is an object with coordinates.

Attacking an entity changed as well. The main objective of the change is to be able to execute a tag from the attack routine if it is successful. Those are small changes to the function.

```
attackEntity: function (attacker, victim, weapon) {
    attacker.moving = true
    attacker.tweens = attacker.tweens || 0
    attacker.tweens += 1

    let rangedAttack = weapon.range() ? weapon.attackTile : ↵
    false
    let tint = weapon.range() && weapon.tint ? weapon.tint : ↵
    false
```

The signature for the function changed. Now the weapon is part of the function call. Both the basic enemy and the basic hero were patched to pass the weapon when they call `attackEntity`. Once the function starts, we create the same variables we had before `rangedAttack` and tint, and the body of the function remains basically the same with just two small tweaks.

The dungeon.log call that displays information about the attack has been changed both in the melee attack and the ranged attack to contain the weapon name. In both cases, the new code is

```
this.log(`${attacker.name} does ${damage} damage to ↵
${victim.name} with ${weapon.name}.`)
```

An addition was made in both cases on the immediate line after that log call.

```
weapon.executeTag("damagedEntity", victim)
```

The reason for that change is so that we can have tags such as *#burning* that when applied to a sword would cause `addTag(burning)` to the victim of a successful attack. Prior to this example, the entities had no way to figure out if their call to `attackEntity` succeeded or not. This made hard for tags to cause effects upon being used during attacks. This new `damageEntity` handler will be called for tags that implement it, allowing tags a chance to cause some side effect to the victim of an attack.

Creating tags

Finally, we are able to start working on the tags themselves. Some of our tags will be flexible and provide a different behavior depending on whether they are applied to an item, weapon, enemy, or the player. Others will have a single focus and serve as pluggable behavior or characteristics to give the game flavor or behavior to monsters. A folder called `tags/` will host all the tags, and each tag will be their own file.

Making monsters more aggressive

The aggro tag is inside `tags/aggro.js`; it only causes an effect on enemies and makes them more aggressive by giving them more actions per turn. So if an enemy would attack the player once per turn, an aggressive enemy will attack three times.

```
const aggro = {
    name: "Aggro",
    initialize: function () {
        if (this.type === "enemy") {
```

```
        this.tint = 0x00bc00
        this.refreshRates.actionPoints += 2

        if (this.sprite) {
            this.sprite.tint = this.tint
            this.sprite.tintFill = true
        }
      }
    }
  }
}
```

```
export default aggro
```

This is a good example of a tag that just alters those values set by the monster constructors. As we know, when a tag is applied to an entity, its initialize function is executed. In the aggro tag, we check to see if the tag is being applied to an enemy, and if it is, we do some cosmetic changes and then increase the amount of action points that entity has.

The idea about doing different tints depending on the tag is twofold: on one side, the game gets more interesting; on another, it becomes easier to debug because you can see the same tint on the map and on the sidebar, making it easier to match the user interface in the sidebar with the entities on the map.

Previously, we initialized a skeleton like

```
tm.addEntity(new Skeleton(x,y))
```

Now, we could do

```
tm.addEntity(new enemies.Skeleton(x,y).addTags(["aggro"]))
```

And initialize an aggressive skeleton.

Making fast monsters

Inside tags/fast.js, you will find the code for this tag.

```
const fast = {
    name: "Fast",
    initialize: function () {
        if (this.type === "enemy") {
            this.tint = 0x00bb00
            this.refreshRates.movementPoints += 2

            if (this.sprite) {
                this.sprite.tint = this.tint
                this.sprite.tintFill = true
            }
        }
    }
}

export default fast
```

It is quite similar to the aggro tag, but instead of increasing the actionPoints, it increases the movementPoints.

What about golden things?

Roguelikes are full of golden stuff, right? The tags/golden.js is our first flexible tag.

```
import dungeon from "../dungeon.js"

const golden = {
    name: "Golden",
    initialize: function () {
        this.name = `Golden ${this.name}`
        this.tint = 0xccbc00
```

```
    if (this.sprite) {
        this.sprite.tint = this.tint
        this.sprite.tintFill = true
    }

    if (this.type == "item") {
        this.equipHPBonus = 1
    }
},
```

The golden tag is flexible only when taken into account that it has different effects depending on the item it is applied to. If that tag is applied to an entity that is not an item, then all the changes are purely cosmetic.

If the tag is added to an item, we set a special equipHPBonus variable whose use will become clear in the next part of the code.

```
equip(acc, itemNumber, entity) {
    if (this.equipHPBonus > 0) {
        dungeon.log(`+${this.equipHPBonus} health bonus ⏎
        for equipping golden item.`)
        entity.healthPoints += this.equipHPBonus
        this.equipHPBonus = 0
    }
},
```

The tag overrides the equip function. Equipping a golden item will cause the item's default equip function to run and then this equip function to run afterward. In the equip function, we check to see if that property we set in the initialize function is larger than zero. If it is, then we increase the entity (aka the player) healthPoints by the same amount we set in that property during the tag initialization.

You may be wondering if equip always passed the entity as an argument. It didn't; I added that in this chapter. It is a single word change to the basic hero so that toggleItem now uses equip(itemNumber, this) instead of the previous version that used equip(itemNumber).

```
attack(acc = 0) {
    if (acc > 0) {
        acc += 1
    }
    return acc
},
```

Changes made to attack affect only weapons because attack will be called with the value returned by the item's own attack function as a parameter. Nonweapons always return zero from that function, so our golden tag only increases the attack for weapons.

```
    protection(acc = 0) {
        if (acc > 0) {
            acc += 1
        }
        return acc
    }
}
```

```
export default golden
```

Exactly the same with protection, normal items and weapons return zero when protection is called. Some defensive items such as shields return a positive value. In that case, the value is increased.

We might as well have a silver tag

Inside tags/silver.js, you'll find the code for the silver tag. Like in most games, silver is less valuable than gold, so this tag does less.

```
import dungeon from "../dungeon.js"

const silver = {
    name: "Silver",
    initialize: function () {
        this.name = `Silver ${this.name}`
        this.tint = 0xccbc00

        if (this.sprite) {
            this.sprite.tint = this.tint
            this.sprite.tintFill = true
        }

        if (this.type == "item") {
            this.equipHPBonus = 2
        }
    },

    equip(acc, itemNumber, entity) {
        if (this.equipHPBonus > 0) {
            dungeon.log(`+${this.equipHPBonus} health bonus ↵
            for equipping silver item.`)
            entity.healthPoints += this.equipHPBonus
            this.equipHPBonus = false
        }
    }
}

export default silver
```

It doesn't provide either attack or protection bonuses, but it gives the entity a larger healthPoints bonus than the golden tag.

And an iron tag as well

The iron tag is in tags/iron.js, and it is the opposite of the silver tag when compared to the golden tag. Silver is just healthPoints bonus, and iron is just attack and protection bonuses.

```
const iron = {
    name: "Iron",
    initialize: function () {
        this.name = `Iron ${this.name}`
        this.tint = 0xccbc00

        if (this.sprite) {
            this.sprite.tint = this.tint
            this.sprite.tintFill = true
        }
    },

    attack(acc = 0) {
        if (acc > 0) {
            acc += 1
        }
        return acc
    },
```

```
    protection(acc = 0) {
        if (acc > 0) {
            acc += 1
        }
        return acc
    }
}

export default iron
```

Making enemies royal

I had this silly dream of applying a tag to a skeleton and making it Lord
Skeletah which would be terrifying. Making an enemy royal gives it a lot
of bonuses and changes its name to something whimsical. Inside tags/
royal.js is the source for this tag.

```
const royal = {
    name: "Royal",
    initialize: function () {
        if (this.type === "enemy") {
            this.tint = 0xccbc00
            this.refreshRates.actionPoints += 2
            this.refreshRates.movementPoints += 2
            this.refreshRates.healthPoints += 1

            if (this.sprite) {
                this.sprite.tint = this.tint
                this.sprite.tintFill = true
            }
```

```
        let title = Phaser.Utils.Array.GetRandom([ ↵
        "Count", "Duke", "Lord", "Duchess", "Baron",
        "Baroness", "Countess"])
        let suffix = Phaser.Utils.Array.GetRandom([ ↵
        "ah", "oz", "von", "zits", "gres"])
        this.name = `${title} ${this.name.slice(0,this. ↵
        name.length-2)}${suffix}`
    }
  }
}

export default royal
```

Most of the source is just playing with strings to come up with funny royal names for the enemies, but among all that random array picking and string manipulation, the enemy is having all its refresh rates increased. Oh, and royal enemies heal over time.

Entering a dungeon and finding an enemy that is at the same time royal and hunting for you is quite dangerous.

Making a flexible burning tag

Like the others, the burning tag is in tags/burning.js. This tag exemplifies the idea of a flexible tag for me. There is a huge difference between yielding a flaming sword and actually being in flames, as any fan of *Game of Thrones* will be able to tell.

A burning tag on an item will cause it to spread into entities every time an attack with that item is successful.

If the burning tag is on a monster or the player, then they suffer damage every turn for a couple number of turns or until the tag is removed by removeTag.

```
import dungeon from "../dungeon.js"

const burning = {
    name: "Burning",
    initialize: function (damage = 2, howManyTurns = 3) {
        this._burnDamage = damage
        this._howManyTurns = howManyTurns
        if (this.type === "item") {
            this.tint = 0x002300

            if (this.sprite) {
                this.sprite.tint = this.tint
                this.sprite.tintFill = true
            }
        }
    },
},
```

This is our first tag to have potential arguments in the initialize function. We're not going to use them at the moment and will rely on their default value, but by having them there, we're setting up the opportunity to have devastating fire on the game.

The damage caused by burning will last howManyTurns and will cause damage amount of damage to the entity.

Since it causes an effect every turn, it has its own implementation of the turn function.

```
turn() {
    if (this.type !== "item") {
        if (this._howManyTurns > 0 && !this._burningActivated) {
            this._burningActivated = true
            this.healthPoints -= this._burnDamage
            this._howManyTurns -= 1
```

```
            dungeon.log(`${this.name} suffers ↵
            ${this._burnDamage} hits from burning.`)
        }

        if (this._howManyTurns == 0) {
            this.removeTag(burning)
        }
    }
},
```

When implementing this type of side effect, we need to remember that the turn function is called multiple times in a given turn. It is like the Phaser update function being called in a cycle until the player's turn is over. If this tag simply caused damage on each turn invocation, the player would die even before their first turn was over as Phaser might call the turn function multiple times per second.

The solution to that is to have a flag that is checked during the turn before applying damage. This flag is only reverted during refresh, which is a function that is called only once per turn, thus making sure that we only cause damage once per turn. After howManyTurns have passed, the tag is removed.

```
refresh() {
    this._burningActivated = false
},
```

Refresh just flips that tag so that the next invocation of turn causes damage. Talking about damage, the next function is damageEntity. This function is called when a successful attack is made and the entity argument it receives is the victim of the attack.

```
damagedEntity(entity) {
    entity.addTag(burning)
    return entity
}

}

export default burning
```

When damageEntity is called, the fire spreads to the other entity (the victim) and will cause it harm for howManyTurns.

Making stuff poisonous

The poison tag, which is in tags/poison.js, has the same implementation as the burning tag. The only differences are in the name and cosmetics and the values for damage and howManyTurns. Burning causes two points of damage for three turns, while poison causes one point of damage for ten turns.

Things can be cursed too

Another variation on the same tag implementation is cursed, which is in tags/cursed.js; it causes one damage for five turns but besides that remains the same as the others.

Making enemies move

It is time to create the tags that will govern the enemies' behaviors. Unlike the previous tags we've implemented so far, these tags can't be applied multiple times to a given enemy. Each enemy is supposed to have one and only one monster behavior tag. What these tags will do is provide the monster with a turn implementation.

The hunter

Our previous skeleton implementation acted like this. It figured out where the player was anywhere in the dungeon, plotted a path toward them, and hunted the player until it was dead. For the hunter tag, tags/hunter.js, we will abstract that behavior into a self-contained tag.

```
import dungeon from "../dungeon.js"

const hunter = {
    name: "Hunter",
    initialize: function () {
        if (this.type === "enemy") {
            this.tint = 0xe3e3e3

            if (this.sprite) {
                this.sprite.tint = this.tint
            }
        }
    },
```

Nothing really interesting is happening in the initialization. It is more about color-coding the sprite so that we can find them on the map than anything else.

```
    turn() {
        let oldX = this.x
        let oldY = this.y
        let pX = dungeon.player.x
        let pY = dungeon.player.y
        let grid = new PF.Grid(dungeon.level)
        let finder = new PF.AStarFinder()
        let path = finder.findPath(oldX, oldY, pX, pY, grid)
```

```
    if (this.movementPoints > 0) {
        if (path.length > 2) {
            dungeon.moveEntityTo(this, path[1][0], ⏎
            path[1][1])
        }

        this.movementPoints -= 1
    }

    if (this.actionPoints > 0) {
        if (dungeon.distanceBetweenEntities(this, ⏎
        dungeon.player) <= 2) {
            dungeon.attackEntity(this, dungeon.player, ⏎
            this.weapon)
        }

        this.actionPoints -= 1
    }
  }
}

export default hunter
```

The turn implementation is a copy and paste from the previous skeleton. It finds the player, plots a path to them, and, if near enough, will attack them. The attackEntity call has been amended to pass the weapon being used.

Monsters that are going somewhere

If every enemy in the dungeon is a hunter, then the game can quickly become a mob. This tag, located in tags/goingSomewhere.js, allows us to create a monster that, at first glance, doesn't actually care for the player at all.

When a monster is going somewhere, they select a random location in the map and start moving toward each every turn. Once they reach their destination, they select another random tile and the process repeats. Only if the player passes near them that they notice them and change their destination to be the player.

```
import dungeon from "../dungeon.js"

const goingSomewhere = {
    name: "Going Somewhere",
    initialize: function () {
        if (this.type === "enemy") {
            this.tint = 0xdd0000

            if (this.sprite) {
                this.sprite.tint = this.tint
                this.sprite.tintFill = true
            }
        }
    },
```

It's another uninspiring initialization, just some tint to help us figure out which enemies are doing what.

```
turn() {
    let oldX = this.x
    let oldY = this.y
    let dX = this._destinationX
    let dY = this._destinationY

    if (!dX || !dY ) {
        let randomCoords = dungeon.randomWalkableTile()
        this._destinationX = randomCoords.x
        this._destinationY = randomCoords.y
```

```
        dX = this._destinationX
        dY = this._destinationY
    }
```

Primarily, the entity needs to select a destination tile. That is what is done by the first if clause earlier.

```
if (oldX == dX && oldY == dY) {
    // arrived at destination, find new target.
    let randomCoords = dungeon.randomWalkableTile()
    this._destinationX = randomCoords.x
    this._destinationY = randomCoords.y
    dX = this._destinationX
    dY = this._destinationY
}
```

If the entity arrived at their destination, then they select a new destination and start moving again.

```
console.log(`${this.name} going to ${dX},${dY}`)

let grid = new PF.Grid(dungeon.level)
let finder = new PF.AStarFinder()
let path = finder.findPath(oldX, oldY, dX, dY, grid)

if (this.movementPoints > 0) {
    if (path.length > 1) {
        dungeon.moveEntityTo(this, path[1][0],
        path[1][1])
    }

    this.movementPoints -= 1
}
```

I've added a console.log call to help find out where each enemy with this tag is going. I was tired of chasing them while trying out these tags, and it became easier to plot a path to them if I knew where they were going.

```
// If the player is near, go after them.
if (dungeon.distanceBetweenEntities(this, dungeon.player) <= 5) {
    this._destinationX = dungeon.player.x
    this._destinationY = dungeon.player.y
}
```

If the player is close enough, then move closer. Be aware that this doesn't necessarily make the enemy attack the player or pursue the player like a hunter. If the player moves away, then the enemy will move toward that tile that was previously occupied by the player and then select another destination.

```
    // Attack player if you can
    if (this.actionPoints > 0) {
        if (dungeon.distanceBetweenEntities(this, ↵
        dungeon.player) <= 2) {
            dungeon.attackEntity(this, dungeon.player, ↵
            this.weapon)
        }

        this.actionPoints -= 1
    }
},
```

Only if the player is really close to that enemy that it attacks.

```
  refresh() {
      if (dungeon.distanceBetweenEntities(this, ↵
      dungeon.player) <= 5) {
          dungeon.log(`${this.name} grrrr!!!`)
      }
  }

}

export default goingSomewhere
```

This call to dungeon.log during refresh is just so that the player learns that the entity spotted them and is angry.

Patrolling the dungeon

Inside tags/patrolling.js, you'll find a variation of the going somewhere tag. While that tag selects a tile at random, moves to it, and, upon reaching its destination, selects a new random tile, the patrolling tag moves a monster from its starting position in the dungeon to a random selected tile back and forth. When it reaches the destination tile, it goes back toward its starting tile, rinse, repeat.

It does that by keeping track of its initial position and its destination position.

```
import dungeon from "../dungeon.js"

const patrolling = {
    name: "Patrolling",
    initialize: function () {
        if (this.type === "enemy") {
            this.tint = 0xdd00cd
```

```
        if (this.sprite) {
            this.sprite.tint = this.tin
            this.sprite.tintFill = true
        }

        this._initialX = this.x
        this._initialY = this.y

        let randomCoords = dungeon.randomWalkableTile()
        this._destinationX = randomCoords.x
        this._destinationY = randomCoords.y

        this._targetX = this._destinationX
        this._targetY = this._destinationY
    }
},
```

The initial position is kept in this._initialX and this._initialY; the destination tile coordinates are kept in this._destinationX and this._destinationY. One of those two sets of coordinates will be copied to this._targetX and this._targetY which is the goal for the entity movement.

The implementation of turn is remarkably similar to the going somewhere implementation, but instead of selecting a new random spot, it just flips between the starting position and a preselected random destination.

```
turn() {
        let oldX = this.x
        let oldY = this.y

        if (oldX == this._initialX && oldY == this._initialY) {
            // arrived at destination, find new target.
            this._targetX = this._destinationX
```

```javascript
        this._targetY = this._destinationY
    }

    if (oldX == this._destinationX && oldY == ↵
    this._destinationY) {
        this._targetX = this._initialX
        this._targetY = this._initialY
    }

    console.log(`${this.name} patrolling to ↵
    ${this._targetX},${this._targetY}`)

    let grid = new PF.Grid(dungeon.level)
    let finder = new PF.AStarFinder()
    let path = finder.findPath(oldX, oldY, this._targetX, ↵
    this._targetY, grid)

    if (this.movementPoints > 0) {
        if (path.length > 1) {
            dungeon.moveEntityTo(this, path[1][0], ↵
            path[1][1])
        }

        this.movementPoints -= 1
    }

    // If the player is near, go after them.
    if (dungeon.distanceBetweenEntities(this, ↵
    dungeon.player) <= 5) {
        this._targetX = dungeon.player.x
        this._targetX = dungeon.player.y
    }
```

```
    // Attack player if you can
    if (this.actionPoints > 0) {
        if (dungeon.distanceBetweenEntities(this, ↵
        dungeon.player) <= 2) {
            dungeon.attackEntity(this, dungeon.player, ↵
            this.weapon)
        }

        this.actionPoints -= 1
    }
},
```

Depending on how long the path selected during the tag initialization, the player might learn the movements of the monster and avoid it. If a strong monster is patrolling, then the player can avoid combat by being stealthy and walking around it.

```
refresh() {
    if (dungeon.distanceBetweenEntities(this, ↵
    dungeon.player) <= 5) {
        dungeon.log(`${this.name} raaawwrr!!!`)
    }
}

}

export default patrolling
```

Creating the tags module

All the parts are done, and we can implement the tags module, whose source code is inside tags.js. This module is made in the same image as the enemies and items modules.

Besides exporting all the available tags, this module exports functions to retrieve a random monster and to retrieve a random item.

```
import aggro from "./tags/aggro.js"
import fast from "./tags/fast.js"
import goingSomewhere from "./tags/goingsomewhere.js"
import patrolling from "./tags/patrolling.js"
import golden from "./tags/golden.js"
import iron from "./tags/iron.js"
import silver from "./tags/silver.js"
import hunter from "./tags/hunter.js"
import poison from "./tags/poison.js"
import burning from "./tags/burning.js"
import royal from "./tags/royal.js"
import cursed from "./tags/cursed.js"
```

It begins by importing every single tag.

```
const tags = {
    aggro,
    fast,
    goingSomewhere,
    golden,
    silver,
    iron,
    hunter,
    poison,
    burning,
    royal,
    patrolling,
    cursed
}
```

It assembles an object to be exported with all the tags. After that, we create specialized arrays containing tags that cover a specific domain.

```
export const materials= [
    "golden",
    "silver",
    "iron"
]
```

Materials are tags that modify the nature of the item.

```
export const enemyModifiers = [
    "aggro",
    "fast",
    "royal"
]
```

Enemy modifiers are bonuses that are applied to a monster.

```
export const behaviors = [
    "goingSomewhere",
    "hunter",
    "patrolling"
]
```

Behaviors are only applicable to enemies; they will provide the turn function implementation.

```
export const effects = [
    "poison",
    "burning",
    "cursed"
]
```

Effects are tags that cause a side effect at every turn.

```
export function getRandomTagsForItem(modifierCount = 1, ↵
effectCount = 0) {
    let res = new Set()

    while (modifierCount > 0) {
        res.add(Phaser.Utils.Array.GetRandom(materials))
        modifierCount--
    }

    while (effectCount > 0) {
        res.add(Phaser.Utils.Array.GetRandom(effects))
        effectCount--
    }

    return [...res]
}
```

That function returns an array to be used with addTags on an item. It does so by selecting a number of tags from the materials and the effects. A set is used so that the same tag is not applied more than once.

```
export function getRandomTagsForEnemy(modifierCount = 1) {
    let res = new Set()

    while (modifierCount > 0) {
        res.add(Phaser.Utils.Array.GetRandom(enemyModifiers))
        modifierCount--
    }

    res.add(Phaser.Utils.Array.GetRandom(behaviors))

    return [...res]
}

export default tags
```

The corresponding function for getting an array of tags that are applicable to an enemy is very similar except that we're not applying materials or effects. Monsters get enemyModifiers and one behavior.

With a final refactor to the world scene, we're ready to test all these additions.

Refactoring the world scene

Instead of hardcoding the monsters and their positions in the world scene (which lives in world.js), we're going to refactor it to use random items and monsters in random locations.

First, we need to change the imports to pick the new modules.

```
import dungeon from "./dungeon.js"
import tm from "./turnManager.js"
import classes from "./classes.js"
import { getRandomItem } from "./items.js"
import { getRandomEnemy } from "./enemies.js"
```

The next required change is simple; just remove all that block of code that adds the skeletons and items from the create function. After the player is created, add the following:

```
dungeon.player = new classes.Elf(15, 15)

tm.addEntity(dungeon.player)
let  monsterCount= 10
while(monsterCount> 0) {
    let tile = dungeon.randomWalkableTile()
    tm.addEntity(getRandomEnemy(tile.x, tile.y))
    monsterCount--
}
```

```
let itemCount = 10
while(itemCount > 0) {
    let tile = dungeon.randomWalkableTile()
    tm.addEntity(getRandomItem(tile.x, tile.y))
    itemCount--
}
```

That will create ten monsters and ten items in random positions on the dungeon. Try playing a couple times in it.

Procedural generation is not just throwing random things

If I may use an analogy here, what we've done so far in this chapter is like wanting to go on a boat tour, climbing into the boat, and then without sail, motor, or oars, just letting it randomly take you anywhere. It might be fun, but you're not really in control of what is going on.

Procedural generation is about using randomness to steer the game into the direction you want while keeping the content fresh and increasing the game replayability. At this point in the source, we are like those thousand monkeys with typewriters and infinite time. There might be a Shakespeare play in the end, but during the middle of the process, it is all quite chaotic.

Phaser has functions to retrieve random items with a bias toward the beginning of the array – that function is called `weightedPick`[4] – this allows you a simple but effective way of biasing the results. If you use that function with an array like

```
["skeleton", "skeleton", "skeleton", "bat", "bat", "orc"]
```

---

[4]WeightedPick documentation: `https://photonstorm.github.io/phaser3-docs/Phaser.Math.RandomDataGenerator.html#weightedPick__anchor`

the dungeon will be biased toward spawning skeletons and bats. The same can be used to make most monsters into *patrolling* and *going somewhere* instead of hunters (that are more dangerous).

Applying this function to tag selection is also a good idea. The royal tag should be rare, and most items don't actually need a tag. Having an array like

```
[false, false, false, "iron", "iron", "silver", "golden"]
```

would make most of the items untagged. With the default values for the arguments of getRandomTagsForItem, it is impossible to get an effect in the array. A biased approach could make the effects rare by default.

And that is just by exploring a single function – the weightedPick – Phaser offers other useful functions in its Phaser.Utils.Array[5] namespace that can be used to craft bespoke algorithms for making decisions upon procedural generation. You could change the bias of the game depending on how powerful the player is; you can factor the time of the day, making your game harder during the evening. It is your call.

Just remember that the code we've been building here is not biased; I mean it is under a bias that we control, it is just random, and that doesn't make for a good game. The values for the entity properties such as damage, points, and all the rest have not been playtested and through a real quality assurance process. At this moment in the source, we're having fun, but unless you take control over the source and direct the procedural generation and the play experience toward the game you desire, you won't make a good or memorable game.

---

[5]Phaser.Utils.Array documentation: https://photonstorm.github.io/phaser3-docs/Phaser.Utils.Array.html

Exercises

This has been a huge chapter. There is a lot of potential for being creative with tags, so before moving on, can you

- Create a vegan behavior tag?

- Add bias to the functions that return random items and monsters, and make the game easier or harder based on the player class?

- Can you create a necromancer (a monster that depending on what happens can spawn undead skeletons to help them)?

Summary

In this chapter, we've explored a tagging system that enables us to create composable units of code that can be combined and recombined to generate all sorts of items and enemies.

Before moving to the next chapter, make sure you

- Understand how the Taggable class work

- Have a clear grasp about how each tag behaves and how useful they are

- Have experimented with different biases by fiddling with the code and the random generation routines

In the next chapter, we will dive deep into generating new dungeons and add a bit of bias to the game.

CHAPTER 8

Procedurally Generated Dungeons

For many people, procedurally generated dungeons are one of the main defining characteristics of the roguelike genre, if not the most important one. Because of that, there is a lot of work, lore, and techniques developed in the last decades covering this topic, and it would be impractical for an introductory book such as this one to cover a significant part of the techniques available to roguelike developers. Instead, we're going to focus on one type of dungeon generation that is easy to understand and experiment with while just describing others without implementing them. It is important to understand that even though the algorithm behind the dungeon generation explained in this chapter is easy, it is a battle-tested way of generating dungeons with many games using it.

Learning how to do dungeon generation in this chapter is an initial step to think about dungeon generation in general and how to implement novel ways of doing it or tweaking some existing algorithm toward some intention you have. As your game development path progresses, you'll learn more complex ways of doing it and experiment with advanced techniques that are beyond what I can include here, but even when you reach those more refined steps in your journey, you'll always be able to come back to what was learned here and still use it.

© Andre Alves Garzia 2020
A. A. Garzia, *Roguelike Development with JavaScript*,
https://doi.org/10.1007/978-1-4842-6059-3_8

Dungeons, fun, and replayability

Dungeon generation, and procedural generation in general, is not about chaos and randomness. If all you do is throw random parameters into some set of functions waiting for something beautiful to exit through the other end, you're no different than someone just throwing mud on a wall until, maybe, it forms a recognizable figure. To be honest, throwing mud at a wall might actually be what you want to do; that is OK. I'm not against doing it; I'm just saying it needs to be your intention and not something that happens because you have no control over the process.

The keyword to reason about dungeon generation is *intention*. You are going to craft an algorithm that with the aid of some input generates a dungeon for your game. You want these dungeons to have some feel to it, may it be in the way they are designed or the challenges they will provide; whatever it is that makes those dungeons *your dungeons*, there must be an intention behind it. At this learning stage, it is OK to just pick a generic algorithm and use it much like a market-bought, bulk made ready-made meal. Many people in time develop their own custom additions to ready-made meals; if you just check the Internet for ways to improve ready-made instant ramen, you'll find a whole subculture of recipes out there. The same happens with game development algorithms; you have the ready-made stuff that you can just plug into your game and use. We did that with our pathfinding algorithm, but it pays off to fiddle with those ready-made packages and try to come up with something that has your mark on them.

Fiddling with algorithms is not only a way to imprint your own personal creativity into the process but a way to understand that algorithm better. Especially when you accidentally break everything, put on your computer forensic hat, and go on to debug it.

The end game can be summarized as trying to come up with fun-to-play dungeons. What that means to you and your players might be different than what other players and developers mean when they say that a given dungeon is fun. Some people are attracted to fiendishly levels of difficulty and dungeons that challenge them in every step of the way; others want interesting visuals and are more attracted to the immersive quality of the game and the world that unfolds before them. A good practice for this chapter is to play some runs of the dungeons we'll generate and try to figure out what you find fun and rewarding and then tweak the code to be more like that.

Another key aspect is replayability; procedurally generated dungeons and content provide a maximum of replayability, allowing gamers to have eternal fun with the game. But procedural generation has limits, and maybe whatever you are doing can only generate dungeons with a certain feel, and after a while even though the corridors and rooms are different, they are all recognizable, and the game no longer feels as fun as it did. That is OK because the fun of a game doesn't rely only on its dungeon generation but on the sum of its gaming experience, and maybe the dungeon doesn't actually play a large role in your game. Dungeons generated with the technique described in this chapter will be like that; they will all be quite similar to one another, so to keep the game fresh, we'll need to figure out what to do with it. It's not unlike having a fixed set of ingredients and trying to come up with new recipes; it can work.

Being *fun and replayable* is probably one of the favorite feedback that a roguelike developer can receive from a player. In my opinion, the key factor for replayability is to have procedural generation that is stable and well understood by the developers. Unless that is in place, the game can end up generating broken dungeons, thus spoiling that run of the game. I was playing a popular console roguelike, and it generated a beautiful dungeon but placed my character in a position it couldn't move. I was locked in place wondering how that edge case has not been taken care of.

Bugs happen in any codebase, and when dealing with procedural generation, we need to be aware not only of bugs in our code but bugs generated by the runtime output of our code; it is a tricky business and we can forgive and understand edge cases. I just rebooted the game, and the next run was fine except for the fact that I died rather quickly for something that looked like a toad, very shameful. Replayability is a side effect of being in control of your algorithms. There is no replayable game, which I am aware of, where the developers are not on top of their procedural generation.

Fun is harder to measure and reason about, but I believe it comes down to the balancing act between realizing and subverting expectations. If all you do is subvert the player expectation, your game soon becomes the equivalent of bland jump-scare movies. You'll definitely surprise people, but they might not find it enjoyable. If all you do is fulfill expectation, then it becomes just bland, not memorable, not fun. You can still do it because sometimes all you need is to go through the motions of the game while thinking about something else, but you probably won't recommend that game to someone else.

The little game we've been building is more of an exercise, so it has a lot of this bland fulfillment I just spoke about. To create the kind of experience we love in roguelikes requires time, QA, and playtest, beyond what we can do in book sample code. Still, we can point out where the code could be made more fun and where good understanding might improve replayability.

Among all procedurally generated content you have in your roguelike, dungeon generation is probably what your gamers will first notice. It is the greeting card of your game, the invitation to explore. Instead of shooting for the moon in this chapter, we're going to play it safe and do it in a very classical way. Our dungeon generation will be understandable, easy to tinker with, and most importantly *hard to screw up*.

How to screw up dungeons

Let's begin not by going deep into algorithms but by pondering a bit on what we don't want in our dungeons. Assuming our game is a classical roguelike where a hero descends into many levels of challenges and mayhem trying to fulfill some quest objective, how could we have bad dungeons? By bad dungeons, I'm talking solely about the layout of the dungeon, not about what goes inside it once the layout is set.

A bad dungeon contains nontraversable areas, meaning there are places in which there is no way for the player to get into. I'm not saying that there are places in which the player needs to solve a puzzle, or go through some challenge to get into, or even places that are placed in the game just for aesthetical pleasure and in which the player is not supposed to go. I'm talking about having rooms in the dungeon layout that the player should be able to go but can't because the layout of wherever the player is located doesn't have any possible path connection to that room; the stuff that happens when you plug that A^* algorithm into it disregarding any blockers such as doors, monsters, and so on, and it still replies with a *null path*. We must make sure our level is traversable.

Another screw up, one that might just be a screw up in my own personal opinion and not be significant to other people, is when the entrance and the exit of a level are just too close, basically allowing an express way down for the player. This is less of a problem, as anyone who played through dungeons that were generated this way can quickly attest that going down fast makes you arrive at more dangerous monsters with a less powerful character. Still, for me, it saps a bit of the fun part of it, especially the suspense. Whenever I go down a set of stairs as a player, I'm always wondering, how far is the next exit and what lies between me and it? In our algorithm, we're going to aim to place the entrance and exit points at some decent distance from one another. It will not be infallible, but it will not simply be random.

That is our mantra for the chapter: traversable dungeons in which the player needs to traverse a number of rooms before moving on. The tool we'll use to build our dungeons is called *binary space partitioning* (BSP).

Using BSP to build dungeons

Binary space partitioning is a technique for dividing spaces into smaller spaces using recursion. The spaces generated by this technique are all *convex*, which means that given two points in this space, you can't plot a line from one to the other that steps outside of the designated space. The mathematical and computer science research and applications behind it are all very interesting, and if you're inclined toward this kind of subject, you should definitely check it out. For our purposes, we're not going to delve too much into the theory and science of it, but instead use it in a very simple way to build dungeons.

What we'll do is assemble a tree structure known as BSP tree. It is a binary tree in which the nodes either have two children, or are at the leaves of the tree. It is a complete tree so all the parents of the leaves have two children.

To assemble such tree, we'll pick the grid we use for the level, decide a random spot on the map, and use it to split the level into two areas, with some constraints so that the areas are not too small. For the second iteration, we'll pick these two areas and split each of them in two at random coordinates inside them, and so on for each iteration. In Figure 8-1, we can see the tree and map after two iterations.

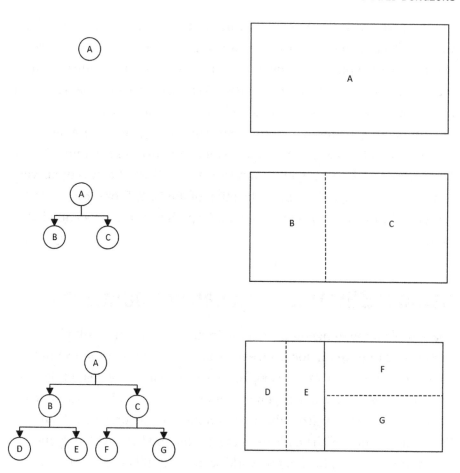

Figure 8-1. *Visualizing a BSP tree*

There is a more thorough description of this process at the RogueBasin[1] website. The algorithm we're going to implement is based on that article and this reference implementation[2] in JS (that implementation uses canvas instead of Phaser).

---

[1]RogueBasin article about BSP Dungeons: www.roguebasin.com/index.php?title=Basic_BSP_Dungeon_generation

[2]BSP Dungeon in JS by Lluis Esquerda: https://eskerda.com/bsp-dungeon-generation/

Once we divide the map into the desired number of areas, we end up with a collection of nonoverlapping rectangles. That is very good because we know we can place a dungeon room inside each of these areas, and they will not intersect with one another. As long as the room being placed in an area is smaller than the area itself, all rooms should fit.

Connecting the rooms is just a matter of walking the *BSP tree* and connecting siblings with a corridor. So for Figure 8-1, we'd connect *D* and *E*, and *F* and *G*, then we would connect *B* and *C*. Once that was done, you can be sure that regardless of the location of the *D*, *E*, *F*, or *G* rooms or the associated corridors, you can always find a path to another location in the dungeon.

Using a BSP tree to generate room areas

I have broken the dungeon generation in this chapter into multiple samples, so that we can focus on each step separately. For this example, please look into `chapter-8/example-1-areas`. Our objective for this first sample is to use a *BSP tree* to generate enough areas to place our rooms.

Instead of working from the final sample from the previous chapter, I've removed most of the code from that folder and left it with only the minimum necessary to load the world scene and still be recognizable as our game. That was a decision made to make the code easier to understand while we're sorting the dungeon generation steps. Once that is done, the final sample for the chapter contains all the code from the previous chapter plus the dungeon generating code.

The parts that have been removed are all the game entity stuff and the user interface sidebar. We don't need to deal with those while sorting how to layout a dungeon map. I've kept other code such as the dungeon module and turn manager because they import one another, and I didn't want to start changing the remaining modules too much just to suit the demo code.

The workflow of the sample remains the same. The game.js file sets the config object for Phaser and loads the world.js scene. The scene loads the dungeon module from dungeon.js and asks dungeon.initialize() to initialize the tilemap. We'll make some alterations to that initialization later in this sample, but first we need to build the necessary code to do all the BSP stuff, so let's start by creating a bspdungeon.js file which will host our dungeon generation code. That code is all self-contained and doesn't need to import anything.

Creating the DNode class

A BSP tree is composed of nodes. To host those nodes, we're creating a new class called DNode (it stands for Dungeon Node). A node needs to keep track of its right and left children nodes (if any) and the area it contains.

```
class DNode {
    constructor(area) {
        this.left = false
        this.right = false
        this.area = area
    }
}
```

It is wise to decouple the node management from the area handling, and that is why we're bundling the area properties inside the node structure. Each node just knows about its potential children and that it contains an area, whatever that may be.

It is safe to assume that we'll need a way to iterate over those areas in the near future, and to do that, we'll need to walk the nodes on this tree. A function called forEachArea was added to this class to help solve that need. That function is an analog of the forEach functions from iterables like array[3] and will execute a *callback* for each area on the tree.

```
forEachArea(f) {
    f(this.area)

    if (this.left) {
        this.left.forEachArea(f)
    }

    if (this.right) {
        this.right.forEachArea(f)
    }
}
}
```

Creating the DArea class

Each DNode will contain a DArea (for Dungeon Area, I was not very inspired when naming these things). The area needs to keep track of its position (its x and y coordinates) and its dimensions (its height and width values).

```
class DArea {
    constructor(x, y, w, h) {
        this.x = x
        this.y = y
```

---

[3]MDN documentation for Array.prototype.forEach: https://developer.mozilla.org/en-US/docs/Web/JavaScript/Reference/Global_Objects/Array/forEach

```
        this.w = w
        this.h = h
    }
}
```

Instead of going full *matryoshka*[4] on this class architecture and placing a room inside every area, we're going to place them dynamically in the next sample. It is important to understand why we're not doing that; it is because only the tree leaves will have rooms, the tree branches won't, so there is no need to place a room property into the DArea class. Due to the nature of our recursive algorithm, the ratio between nodes that have rooms and nodes that shouldn't have rooms doesn't favor placing that property on the class. This is a different situation than the left and right children nodes in a node. Most nodes will have children; only the final nodes (the leaves) won't have children, and that is why those properties were added to the DNode class.

Building a BSP tree

Using the preceding classes, let's add a function called makeTree that, given an initial area and a number of iterations, will recursively split the area using the BSP algorithm. This initial area should be the equivalent of the whole map.

```
function makeTree(area, iterations) {
    let root = new DNode(area)
```

---

[4]More info about Matryoshka dolls: https://en.wikipedia.org/wiki/Matryoshka_doll

```
if (iterations != 0) {
    let [a1, a2] = splitArea(root.area)
    root.left = makeTree(a1, iterations - 1)
    root.right = makeTree(a2, iterations - 1)
}

return root
}
```

At the start, the function creates the root node of the tree, and then it loops calling itself for a number of iterations, splitting the given area and placing each side of the split into the left and right children of the node.

The way this recursive function is built, the final iteration naturally produces the leaves, which are the nodes without children and where our future rooms will be located.

If that let statement looks funny to you, it is because it is using *destructuring assignment*[5] to create a1 and a2 variables with the areas to be placed into the left DNode and right DNode. The nodes don't need to know how those areas are computed, they just need to host them and keep splitting.

The key to this whole project is the function that splits the enclosing area into subareas.

Splitting areas

To split an area, the function will toss a coin and decide if it should split horizontally or vertically. Then it will find either a random X or Y position inside that given area and calculate two subareas based on that coordinate.

---

[5]MDN documentation for destructuring assignments: https://developer.
mozilla.org/en-US/docs/Web/JavaScript/Reference/Operators/
Destructuring_assignment

If we left this algorithm to run as described, it could end up generating areas that are too narrow to contain a room due to the usage of random numbers to pick a coordinate. Instead of constraining the random number generator to values that look OK (but might still be bad), we will calculate either a width-to-height ratio or height-to-width ratio based on the orientation we are splitting the area, and depending on the ratio, we'll discard those values and ask for a new split using recursion.

```
function splitArea(area) {
    let x1, y1, w1, h1 = 0
    let x2, y2, w2, h2 = 0
    if (Phaser.Math.Between(0, 1) == 0) {
        // vertical
        let divider = Phaser.Math.Between(1, area.w)

        x1 = area.x
        y1 = area.y
        w1 = divider
        h1 = area.h

        x2 = area.x + w1
        y2 = area.y
        w2 = area.w - w1
        h2 = area.h

        if (w1 / h1 < 0.45 || w2 / h2 < 0.45) {
            return splitArea(area)
        }
    }
```

The x1, y1, w1, and h1 represent one area, and the x2, y2, w2, and h2 the other area. If the ratio is less than 0.45, then the areas are discarded. Changing that value will change the feel of your areas and is something you can play with. Values between 0.45 and 1.05 appear to yield nice dungeons; below that or above that leads to confusing stuff that is sometimes unusable.

The code for the horizontal split is basically the same, but the calculation for the coordinates is adjusted as needed.

```
    } else {
        // horizontal
        let divider = Phaser.Math.Between(1, area.h)

        x1 = area.x
        y1 = area.y
        w1 = area.w
        h1 = divider

        x2 = area.x
        y2 = area.y + h1
        w2 = area.w
        h2 = area.h - h1

        if (h1 / w1 < 0.45 || h2 / w2 < 0.45) {
            return splitArea(area)
        }
    }

    let a1 = new DArea(x1, y1, w1, h1)
    let a2 = new DArea(x2, y2, w2, h2)

    return [a1, a2]
}
```

By returning an array with the two areas from this function, we can use the destructing assignment in makeTree to cherry-pick those values and assign them to the correct place in the tree.

We now have all the code to do BSP dungeons; we're just missing a dungeon class.

Creating the BSPDungeon generator class

At the end of the multiple iterations of makeTree, the leaves of our tree will contain enough areas to host our rooms. The job of the BSPDungeon class is to pick those areas and output a usable level array to be used by the dungeon module.

If you remember how the level array worked, it was a matrix of Y and X coordinates that contained either a 0 or a 1 depending if the cell was a wall or a walkable tile. We had a hardcoded level stored in a JS file that we have been reusing all throughout the chapters in this book. From this point onward, that level array will be generated at runtime by the BSPDungeon class.

```
export default class BSPDungeon {
    constructor(width, height, iterations) {
        this.rootArea = new DArea(0, 0, width , height )

        this.tree = makeTree(this.rootArea, iterations)

        this.initializeLevelData()

    }
```

A BSPDungeon needs the map dimensions to compute the root area of the BSP tree and how many iterations the BSP process should run for. Once the makeTree function is done, a level data array can be initialized.

```
    initializeLevelData() {
        let lvl = []

        for (let y = 0; y <= this.rootArea.h; y++) {
            lvl[y] = lvl[y] || []
```

```
        for (let x = 0; x <= this.rootArea.w; x++) {
            lvl[y][x] = 0 // empty
        }
    }

    this.levelData = lvl
}
```

The initializeLevelData function makes sure we have a valid level data array with enough cells to host our dungeon map. In this sample, I'm initializing them all to empty so that they don't distract us when rendered to the screen, but once we head back to building an actual game, those tiles will be initialized as walls.

Finally, we add an accessor method to return the level data. This is technically not needed since the code could pluck that data directly from the instance object, but I thought it's better to use such method in case we need to do any extra computation in the future before returning it.

```
toLevelData() {
        return this.levelData
    }
}
```

Changing the world scene

The world scene has been streamlined to contain only the necessary code to render itself without dealing with game entities and the user interface. It begins by importing the new BSPDungeon class, and then it loads the spritesheet data even though we're just setting the tiles to the empty tile at the first position. The update function has been made into a stub that does nothing because we will just render the areas to the screen and not interact with them.

```
import dungeon from "./dungeon.js"
import BSPDungeon from "./bspdungeon.js"

const world = {
    key: "world-scene",
    active: true,
    preload: function () {
        this.load.spritesheet('tiles', ↵
        './assets/colored_transparent.png',
            {
                frameWidth: 16,
                frameHeight: 16,
                spacing: 1
            })
    },
```

The interesting part of that code is the changes made to the create function.

```
    create: function () {
        let dg = new BSPDungeon(80, 50, 4)
        let level = dg.toLevelData()
        dungeon.initialize(this, level)

        let camera = this.cameras.main
        camera.setViewport(0, 0, camera.worldView.width, ↵
        camera.worldView.height)
        camera.setBounds(0, 0, camera.worldView.width, ↵
        camera.worldView.height)
```

We initialize a new BSPDungeon instance with an 80x50 grid and tell the algorithm to iterate over it four times. The resulting level data is passed to the dungeon.initialize() that has been patched to load the level from an argument instead of from a file, a minor tweak. Strictly speaking, the camera setting is not needed by this demo, but we're used to it so I left it there.

The next chunk of that function is the neat one; it will use that forEachArea code to iterate over the areas in the BSPDungeon instance tree and add rectangles to the scene to make them visible.

```
dg.tree.forEachArea(a => {
    let x = dungeon.map.tileToWorldX(a.x)
    let y = dungeon.map.tileToWorldY(a.y)
    let w = a.w * 16
    let h = a.h * 16
    this.add.rectangle(x, y, w, h).setStrokeStyle(4, ↵
    0xff0000, 1, 0.7).setOrigin(0)
})
```

Besides some math to convert between map units to actual pixels, the code is almost a direct correspondence between the area properties and the arguments to create the rectangles. The rectangles are set to transparent, and just their stroke is being set with the setStrokeStyle function call. Don't forget to change the origin point for the graphic to be the top-left corner; the default is the center coordinate, and our math is not really based on that.

Finishing the file is easy:

```
    },
    update: function () {

    }
}

export default world
```

Loading that sample should let you visualize the areas generated by our BSP tree algorithm. Try reloading the page a couple times to see it generating different spaces, and imagine that inside each area, there will be a room.

The image you see will be similar to Figure 8-2, but with different areas since they are procedurally generated.

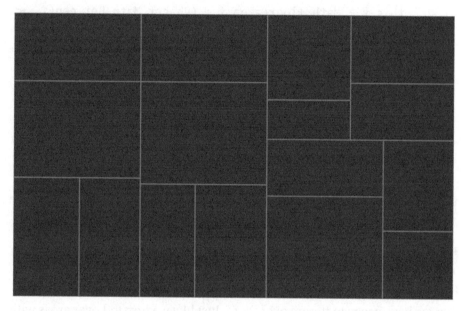

Figure 8-2. *Areas in a dungeon*

It's about time we add some rooms to those areas; let's move to the next sample.

Creating rooms

Our starting point for this sample is the BSPDungeon class. The sample code is inside chapter-8/example-2-rooms/. We need a new class to represent a room; let's call it DRoom.

That class will receive an area in its `constructor` method; this area represents its constraints. We'll use random number generation to decide the position and dimensions of the room, taking care to make them fit inside the given area.

```
class DRoom {
    constructor(area) {
        this.x = Math.floor(area.x + (Phaser.Math.Between(1, ⏎
        area.w) / 3))
        this.y = Math.floor(area.y + (Phaser.Math.Between(1, ⏎
        area.h) / 3))
        this.w = area.w - (this.x - area.x)
        this.h = area.h - (this.y - area.y)
        this.w -= Math.floor(Phaser.Math.Between(1, this.w / 3))
        this.h -= Math.floor(Phaser.Math.Between(1, this.h / 3))
    }
}
```

Iterating over leaves

Rooms will only be located at the leaves of our BSP tree, so it makes sense that we have a way to iterate over them. Just like we iterated over areas with forEachArea, we'll implement a new method inside the DNode class called forEachLeaf.

```
forEachLeaf(f) {
    if (!this.left && !this.right) {
        f(this.area)
    }

    if (this.left) {
        this.left.forEachLeaf(f)
    }
```

```
    if (this.right) {
        this.right.forEachLeaf(f)
    }

}
```

It is just a variation on forEachArea, one that only executes the calling function for leaves. You could make do with just forEachArea and check to see if the node is a leaf in your callback, but why not make things easier and just add the method you need.

Carving rectangles

Once we iterate over each area in a leaf, we need to have a function to be able to carve rectangles in the shape of our rooms. All this function needs to do is flip the cells in the level data that corresponds to our rooms to walkable empty tiles.

Instead of passing a room to this function, we're going to work directly with coordinates and dimensions mostly because it is what the loops inside it will use.

```
fillRect(x, y, w, h, tile) {
    for (let y1 = y; y1 < y + h; y1++) {
        for (let x1 = x; x1 < x + w; x1++) {
            this.levelData[y1][x1] = tile
        }
    }
}
```

Making rooms

By now, we have all the pieces needed to assemble a room. The makeRooms is a method of the BSPDungeon class that iterates over the leaves in the tree, making a room in each of them. To make this more readable, I made it use an auxiliary function inside it instead of coding the callback directly inside the forEachLeaf call.

```
makeRooms() {
    const makeRoom = (area) => {
        area.room = new DRoom(area)
        this.fillRect(area.room.x, area.room.y, ↩
        area.room.w, area.room.h, 0)
    }
    this.tree.forEachLeaf(makeRoom)
}
```

Be aware that we're filling the room rectangles in the level data with zero; that means that we need to flip the initializeLevelData value to one so that the initial array is set to all walls. If we keep it with zero like the previous demo, then our rooms will be invisible because there will be no wall tiles around them.

Adding rooms to the constructor

Patching the constructor for the BSPDungeon is a single line change; just call the makeRooms method after initializing the level data.

```
constructor(width, height, iterations) {
    this.rootArea = new DArea(0, 0, width , height )
```

```
    this.tree = makeTree(this.rootArea, iterations)

    this.initializeLevelData()

    this.makeRooms()
}
```

Loading this sample in your browser should allow you to see both the areas like the previous sample and the rooms in them. It should be similar to Figure 8-3.

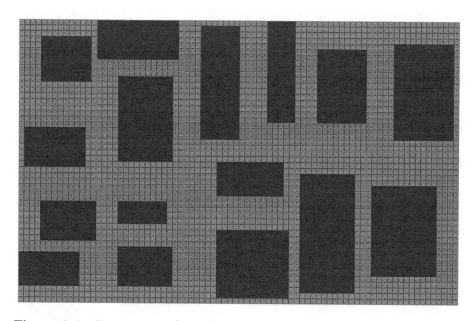

Figure 8-3. *Rooms in a dungeon*

Try reloading the page a couple times and see the variation in the procedural generation. Try playing with those ratios in the splitArea function and see how they affect the dungeon layout.

Our next sample is about connecting those rooms.

Making corridors

Inside chapter-8/example-3-corridors/, you'll find the files for this sample. As you probably thought, all the changes we need for this new sample will be made to the BSPDungeon class.

Making corridors will be a matter of selecting two siblings in the BSP tree, then picking the areas inside them and computing the center of each area. A line of empty walkable tiles is then placed between these two coordinates.

This is an easy to understand approach but a naïve one for it will only work if you're sure your rooms intersect with the center of their areas. The DRoom constructor can be patched to make sure this is the case; this is left as an exercise to the reader.

Making a line in the level data

This function is a method in the BSPDungeon; it is similar to the fillRect method, but it is intended to make a line and not a square so it has a slightly different set of values for its loop.

```
line(x1, y1, x2, y2, tile) {
    for (let y = y1; y <= y2; y++) {
        for (let x = x1; x <= x2; x++) {
            this.levelData[y][x] = tile
        }
    }
}
```

Making a corridor

The new function is quite similar to the makeRooms function; the new method to make corridors will iterate over the BSP tree, making lines between the various sibling areas.

```
makeCorridors() {
    const makePath = (node) => {
        if (node.left && node.right) {
            let x1 = Math.floor(node.left.area.x +
            (node.left.area.w/2))
            let y1 = Math.floor(node.left.area.y +
            (node.left.area.h/2))

            let x2 = Math.floor(node.right.area.x +
            (node.right.area.w/2))
            let y2 = Math.floor(node.right.area.y +
            (node.right.area.h/2))

            this.line(x1, y1, x2, y2, 0)

            makePath(node.left)
            makePath(node.right)
        }
    }
    makePath(this.tree)
}
```

A connected dungeon like Figure 8-4 can be seen when you run this sample.

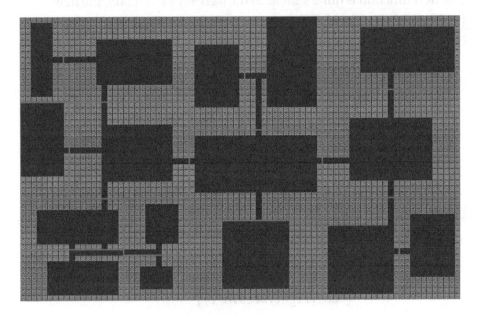

Figure 8-4. *Corridors in a dungeon*

It took a while but we got procedural dungeon layout done. Our dungeons have a blocky feel; all the rooms are square and our corridors straight. It is like our dungeon overlords purchased prefab modules because they were in a hurry, but who am I to judge? That looks good enough for me, and it is time to bring all that back into our game.

A procedurally generated dungeon

Merging the tag sample from the previous chapter and the current work we've done in this chapter is the focus of the new sample located inside chapter-8/example-4-pcg-dungeon/.

The code is the same as the tag sample, but we've added the BSPDungeon class to the folder, patched the dungeon module to receive the level data as an argument, and added an import to the BSPDungeon class at the top of the world scene.

After that, we need to patch the world scene constructor to use the new procedurally generated level data. Be aware that in this sample, we're not adding the colored rectangles, so it is just a matter of initializing the BSPDungeon instance and passing the level data to the dungeon module.

```
create: function () {
        let dg = new BSPDungeon(80, 50, 4)
        let level = dg.toLevelData()
        dungeon.initialize(this, level)

        // Load game entities
        let p = dungeon.randomWalkableTile()
        dungeon.player = new classes.Elf(p.x, p.y)

        tm.addEntity(dungeon.player)
```

Beyond adding the player, all the rest of the code remains the same. Up until building this sample, the player position was hardcoded to be 15x15; now we use a variable p to select a random walkable tile in the dungeon.

In Figure 8-5, you can see how it might look. Were you tired of always using the same map? Those days are over.

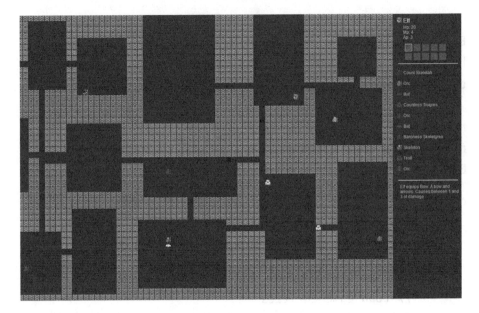

Figure 8-5. *Procedurally generated dungeon*

One cool side effect of making the camera follow the player is that we don't need to worry about the hero character appearing offscreen because the camera will move to make sure they are in view.

It is possible to make this dungeon a little bit better though. I've added an extra sample to this chapter in chapter-8/example-5-better-dungeon/ that changes how items and enemies are placed in the map.

A better dungeon

This is a small variation on the previous sample but an important one. In the previous sample, we just selected random walkable tiles in the dungeon and placed X number of monsters in the level. I don't think that is the best way to do it.

Instead, I've changed the world scene `create` function to loop over rooms and decide what to do for each room. To make this work, first I added a new function to the dungeon module that allowed me to select a random walkable tile inside a room. I've considered just patching the original `randomWalkableTile` function to receive arguments to set constraints, but that would require me to change how some behavior tags work, and I decided to create a new function.

```
randomWalkableTileInRoom: function (x, y, w, h) {
    let rx = Phaser.Math.Between(x, (x + w) - 1)
    let ry = Phaser.Math.Between(y, (y + h) - 1)
    let tileAtDestination = dungeon.map.getTileAt(rx, ry)
    while (typeof tileAtDestination == "undefined" || ↵
tileAtDestination.index == dungeon.sprites.wall) {
        rx = Phaser.Math.Between(x, (x + w) - 1)
        ry = Phaser.Math.Between(y, (y + h) - 1)
        tileAtDestination = dungeon.map.getTileAt(rx, ry)
    }
    return { x: rx, y: ry }
}
```

The changes to the create code in the world scene will not only loop through each room but decide what kind of room it should be. There are empty rooms, rooms with just one monster, rooms with two monsters and one item, and treasure rooms. By relying on `weightedPick`,[6] I can skew the random generation toward empty rooms and rooms with a single monster and make treasure rooms super rare.

---

[6]weightedPick documentation: https://photonstorm.github.io/phaser3-docs/Phaser.Math.RandomDataGenerator.html#weightedPick

A new method getRooms was added to the BSPDungeon class.

```
getRooms() {
    let rooms = []
    this.tree.forEachLeaf(area => {
        rooms.push(area.room)
    })
    return rooms
}
```

This function returns an array that is easy to iterate in the world scene. Another change we're making to that scene is the player's starting position; we're making them start at the leftmost room in the BSP tree. That doesn't mean the leftmost room in the screen but the room contained in the leftmost leaf that was used to generate the dungeon.

```
create: function () {
        let dg = new BSPDungeon(80, 50, 4)
        let level = dg.toLevelData()
        dungeon.initialize(this, level)

        // get rooms
        let rooms = dg.getRooms()

        // Place player in the room at the
        // left-most tree node.
        let node = dg.tree.left
        while (node.left !== false) {
            node = node.left
        }
        let r = node.area.room
        let p = dungeon.randomWalkableTileInRoom(r.x, r.y, ↵
        r.w, r.h)
        dungeon.player = new classes.Elf(p.x, p.y)

        tm.addEntity(dungeon.player)
```

The next step is looping the rooms.

```
rooms.forEach(room => {
    let area = room.w * room.h

    let monsterCount = 0
    let itemCount = 0

    let roomType = Phaser.Math.RND.weightedPick ↵
    ([0,0,0,0,1,1,1,1,1,1,2,2,2,2,3])
```

The weightedPick function returns a random element from the array biased toward the initial elements. By repeating elements, we increase the chances of them happening, especially when adding elements to the beginning of the array.

A switch statement is used to alter how many items and monsters are in each room depending on the value of the roomType variable. Each case in the switch statement will set how many monsters are in the room by setting a value to the mc variable and how many items are there by setting a value to the ic variable.

```
switch (roomType) {
    case 0:
    // empty room.
    monsterCount = 0
    itemCount = 0
    break
    case 1:
    // a monster.
    monsterCount = 1
    itemCount = 0
    break
```

```
        case 2:
        // monster and items.
        monsterCount = 2
        itemCount = 1
        break
        case 3:
        // treasure room.
        monsterCount = 0
        itemCount = 5
        break
    }
```

Once the values are set, we use the same code we had before, a while loop adding entities to the dungeon and turn manager, but instead of using randomWalkableTile, this time we use randomWalkableTileInRoom to place the entities in the correct location.

```
while(mc > 0) {
    let tile = dungeon.randomWalkableTileInRoom ↵
    (room.x, room.y, room.w, room.h)
    tm.addEntity(getRandomEnemy(tile.x, tile.y))
    mc--
}

while(ic > 0) {
    let tile = dungeon.randomWalkableTileInRoom ↵
    (room.x, room.y, room.w, room.h)
    tm.addEntity(getRandomItem(tile.x, tile.y))
    ic--
}
})
```

These changes lead to entity placement that looks more organic.

Exercises

- Try altering the BSPDungeon class using different ratios and see what happens to the dungeon layout.

- Can you make the corridors be in an L or a Z shape instead of straight?

- Come up with different strategies to place monsters and items on the map.

Summary

In this chapter, we worked out how to use procedural generation to generate a dungeon layout. We learned about a common basic technique used by many roguelikes called *binary space partitioning* and how to apply it.

Make sure you understand how the BSPDungeon class works before moving on, and experiment with radically changing it, making sure you start to understand what makes a level fun for you.

In the next chapter, we're going to finish working this sample into a casual roguelike with multiple levels and a winning condition.

CHAPTER 9

Finished Game

Any self-respecting dungeon has more than one level in it. There is no point in digging an underground lair and reusing some eldritch cave structure if you're not going to make it deep. Up to this point in our game, we treated dungeons as a single-level structure because it was easier to code and reason about it. In this chapter, we're going to add multiple levels to the dungeon and create the other scenes necessary for the game introduction, game over, and winning the game. The most complex part is the multiple-level support because it requires refactoring some of our game files.

Adding multiple levels

An easy way to fake our way into multiple levels would be to place stairs into the level and, once the player reaches them, restart the scene which would cause the level to be generated again and appear as a fresh set of rooms and corridors. Even though this approach would look good, it has a problem because it prevents the player from going back to levels they visited before, as reaching the stairs leading up would cause the upward level to be randomized and not be the same as before. Unless your dungeon crawler has a backstory of a dungeon with ever shifting levels, rooms, and corridors that appear to move when you look away, I don't think you'll be able to get away with it.

© Andre Alves Garzia 2020
A. A. Garzia, *Roguelike Development with JavaScript*,
https://doi.org/10.1007/978-1-4842-6059-3_9

Instead, we'll modify our BSP dungeon generator to generate multiple levels at once. We'll shift the dungeon generation and initialization from the world scene and into the dungeon module because we will be restarting both that scene and the UI scene when the player descends or ascends the stairs. The dungeon module is a singleton that can maintain state during these restarts, thus keeping track of the levels, player stats, and location. Other small refactors are needed to the generic game entity classes so that they are able to cope with scene restarts.

The source files for this sample are in `chapter-9/example-1-multiple-levels/`.

Modifying BSPDungeon to support multiple levels

The essence of the change is that we'll rename our old BSPDungeon class to BSPLevel and then create a new BSPDungeon class that, when initialized, creates multiple BSPLevels and keep track of them while providing some features to go up and down and retrieving information about the current level data.

There is an overlap between what we're doing in the dungeon module and what the BSPDungeon class does. They both deal with dungeons and have features to support them; the conceptual difference is that you can replace BSPDungeon with another dungeon generation class and keep using the dungeon module with it. That is why they are separate, so that you can replace one of them without throwing away everything. There are some spots where there is a tight coupling between them; they are not completely independent. This was so the code was easier to understand, but even with that coupling, it is still easier to add new dungeon generation methods than if everything was bundled together on the same file.

Our first step in this refactor is just to rename class BSPDungeon to BSPLevel. With that done, we're ready to code the new BSPDungeon class.

```
export default class BSPDungeon {
    constructor(config) {
        let levels = []

        for (let c = 0; c < config.levels; c++) {
            levels.push(new BSPLevel(config.width, ↵
            config.height, config.iterations))
        }

        this.levels = levels
        this.currentLevel = 0
    }
}
```

The new BSPDungeon class will receive a dungeon configuration object as a parameter. An object as a parameter makes it easier for us to augment the dungeon generation for the next samples in this chapter instead of adding more arguments to the function. The configuration object has the width and height of the dungeon, how many BSP iterations each level should have, and how many levels there are in the dungeon. Most of those parameters are used to initialize the new BSPLevel instances, and the number of levels dictates how many times the level generation loop should go for. A small but important line there is the last one which sets the current level to be the first level of the dungeon. This is where the player will start. Changing that to a higher number will make the player start the game deep into the dungeon, which might be a storytelling feature of your game, for example, you might be doing a game in which the player has been captured and imprisoned in a dungeon and their mission is to escape.

If you remember from the previous samples, the world scene would do direct access to level data from the BSPDungeon instance. This will not work anymore because the class properties changed. What we'll do instead is offer an API to present the same set of data we used before but take into account the currentLevel value.

```
getCurrentLevel() {
    return this.levels[this.currentLevel].toLevelData()
}

getRooms() {
    return this.levels[this.currentLevel].getRooms()
}

getTree() {
    return this.levels[this.currentLevel].tree
}
```

These three methods are analogous to the direct access we used in Chapter 8. The first function, getCurrentLevel, is used to return the level data array to initialize the tilemap. The second function, getRooms, is used to place items and monsters into the level. And the third function, getTree, is used to compute the player position.

All those functions are based on the value of currentLevel. We need to increment or decrement this property when the player goes up or down the stairs.

```
goDown() {
    if (this.currentLevel < this.levels.length - 1) {
        this.currentLevel++
    } else {
        console.error("can't go down, already at the ↵
        bottom of the dungeon.")
    }
}
```

```
goUp() {
    if (this.currentLevel > 0) {
        this.currentLevel--
    } else {
        console.error("can't go up, already at top of the ↵
        dungeon.")
    }
}
```

Both functions are very simple; they just needed some error checking to make sure we don't set the value of currentLevel to numbers that don't make sense.

Letting the dungeon module create the dungeon

As mentioned earlier, we need to shift some of the dungeon creation code out of the world scene and into the dungeon module. When we restart the scene, a procedure needed to move between levels, the create function will run again. We can't have the dungeon generation code there because that would cause the whole set of multiple levels to be regenerated every time the player moves between levels.

Additional code to enable support for multiple levels needs to be implemented as well. The dungeon module will be responsible for starting the process of moving through the stairs, just like it is responsible for movement and combat.

Since we use scene restarts to move through the stairs, it is easier for us to keep track if the dungeon has been initialized or not in the dungeon module than in the world scene. To enable that, we've added an initialized property to the dungeon module object that has a default false value.

```
let dungeon = {
    msgs: [],
    sprites: {
        floor: 0,
        wall: 554,
    },
    initialized: false,
```

Scene restarts will cause dungeon.initialize to be called more than once for a given game session. That function will be called every time the player moves through the stairs and the world scene create function runs. That function will double check the value of the initialized property and only instantiate a new BSPDungeon if it is false. Most of that code has been lifted from the world scene.

```
initialize: function (scene) {
    // create the dungeon only once.
    if (!this.initialized) {
        console.log("dungeon not initialized")
        let dungeonConfig = {
            width: 80,
            height: 50,
            iterations: 4,
            levels: 5
        }
        this.dungeon = new BSPDungeon(dungeonConfig)
        this.initialized = true
    }
}
```

This first block takes care of initializing a BSPDungeon and saving a reference to it.

```
console.log(`dungeon module: current dungeon level`, ↵
this.dungeon.currentLevel)
this.level = this.dungeon.getCurrentLevel()
this.rooms = this.dungeon.getRooms()
this.tree = this.dungeon.getTree()
this.scene = scene
this.levelWithTiles = this.level.map(r => r.map(t => ↵
t == 1 ? this.sprites.wall : this.sprites.floor))

const config = {
    data: this.levelWithTiles,
    tileWidth: 16,
    tileHeight: 16,
}
```

In previous samples, this code was split between the scene and this module; now it is all in one place. We still save references to all the various properties such as rooms and tree because we're leaving the world scene to deal with game entity placement. It will need access to that data there.

```
const map = scene.make.tilemap(config)
const tileset = map.addTilesetImage('tiles', 'tiles', ↵
16, 16, 0, 1)
this.map = map.createDynamicLayer(0, tileset, 0, 0)
},
```

One especially messy characteristic of this codebase is that sprite creation is spread all over the place. Each game entity creates, and saves references to, their own sprites both for placement on the map and on the UI. Moving between levels will require these sprites and references to be disposed of. For most entities, this will just be a side effect of garbage collection and the scene restart not caring about them anymore, but there is one special entity that we're keeping track of and making sure it survives these restarts; that entity is the player.

For the player to survive these restarts, we need it to reset to a state that is similar to its original instantiation but without reinitializing its properties such as healthPoints and actionPoints. We'll deal with that once we start working on the refactor for the basicHero class; what we need to focus on now is the dungeon module. We'll create a cleanup function that calls into these housekeeping functions we'll implement later.

Another important aspect of cleaning up before resetting the scene is making sure the turn manager is empty. We don't want all the entities from the previous level to be littering the next one.

```
cleanup: function () {
    this.msgs = []
    dungeon.player.cleanup()
    tm.cleanup()
},
```

Moving through the stairs will be accompanied by a visual effect to fade the screen to black and then render the new level. When I was implementing this, I've encountered a bug in my code that was due to a misunderstanding on my part about how such functions should work. The camera has a fadeOut function that receives some numerical parameters, telling it how long the fade operation should take and to which color it should fade to, and a callback. I expected this callback to be called at the end of the whole process, but it is actually called for every frame during the fading process, as explained in the fadeOut documentation.[1] That is just a cautionary tale about how sometimes the coding practices that may be familiar to you are not actually how something works in the library you are using. Phaser documentation is very comprehensive and should be explored beyond the links I'm sharing on this book.

---

[1]Camera fadeOut documentation: https://photonstorm.github.io/phaser3-docs/Phaser.Cameras.Scene2D.Camera.html#fadeOut__anchor

The solution is to use an event listener that subscribes to the camerafadeoutcomplete event.

```
goDown: function () {
    this.scene.cameras.main.once('camerafadeoutcomplete', ↵
    () => {
        this.cleanup()
        this.dungeon.goDown()
        this.scene.events.emit('dungeon-changed')
    }, this);
    this.scene.cameras.main.fadeOut(1000, 0, 0, 0);
},
```

It is a bit confusing to have this.dungeon inside the dungeon module. That dungeon property is actually pointing at the instance of the BSPDungeon. I couldn't find another noun to use for that property name. What is happening there is that when the fade is complete, the dungeon module cleans up itself, tells the BSPDungeon to move the currentLevel downward, and emits a custom event.

According to the Phaser documentation, there is more than one way to restart a scene, and searching for this topic on the Internet will yield results with very different ways of doing it (some of which are actually from Phaser 2 and don't work anymore). I've found that the most reliable way of restarting a scene is from inside the scene itself. I couldn't get it to work reliably when I tried doing it from inside the dungeon module. Apparently, the best way to do it is exactly that – send a custom event and let each scene take care of itself. Both the world and the ui scenes will listen for that custom dungeon-changed event. Once it happens, they'll just call their prototype's restart method.

Since we are still reworking the dungeon module, there is something else that will need patching here and in some other files, and that is *input handling*. The only class that deals with input is the basicHero class. Unfortunately, it does that by attaching *input listeners* to the scene. Due to using scene restarts to move through the levels, those input listeners will be discarded when the player goes up or down the dungeon. The player is the only entity that will survive restarts; this means that its constructor will be called only once, at the beginning of the game, and a reference to that entity will be kept and reused after some rinsing for each scene change. Currently, we attach the input listeners from inside the constructors that will change so that we refactor that piece of code into their own separate method; this way, when the player moves between levels, the dungeon module can call that function to set up the listeners again without calling the players constructor.

All that will be explained further once we refactor the player class; right now, what we need to do is change the initializeEntity function in the dungeon module to call the function that will be used to set up those input handlers.

```
initializeEntity: function (entity) {
    if (entity.x && entity.y) {
        let x = this.map.tileToWorldX(entity.x)
        let y = this.map.tileToWorldY(entity.y)
        entity.sprite = this.scene.add.sprite(x, y, ↩
        "tiles", entity.tile)
        entity.sprite.setOrigin(0)
        if (entity.tint) {
            entity.sprite.tint = entity.tint
            entity.sprite.tintFill = true
        }
        entity.setEvents()
    }
},
```

The change was just the final line in which we call entity.set
Events(). This function will be added to the basicHero class, and also to
the genericItem and basicEnemy classes, but in their case, they'll just be
empty stubs.

Our new dungeon module is ready and handling some code that was
formerly from the world scene, which will be the next file we will focus.

Changing the world scene

Some minimal changes are needed to support multiple levels from this
scene; that is because from the point of view of the scene itself, it is always
dealing with just a single dungeon level. Some housekeeping is needed to
remove code that has been copied into the dungeon module, and a listener
for that dungeon-changed needs to be implemented, but besides that, all
the rest remains the same.

Changes to the create function are concentrated at the top; a large part
of it remains the same.

```
create: function () {
    this.events.once('dungeon-changed', () => {
        this.scene.restart()
    })
```

First, before anything else, in the create function, we're registering an
event listener for the custom dungeon-changed event. There isn't much to
do inside besides calling restart; all the rest of the housekeeping needs
were handled by the dungeon module.

```
dungeon.initialize(this)
```

The signature of the initialize method has changed since the world
scene doesn't handle the dungeon generation anymore. Those features are
now handled by the dungeon module.

In the following, we use the new properties we've set up so that we don't need to change much of the code we used to place the player in the dungeon.

```
// get rooms
let rooms = dungeon.rooms

// Place player in the room at the
// left-most tree node.
let node = dungeon.tree.left
while (node.left !== false) {
    node = node.left
}
let r = node.area.room
let p = dungeon.randomWalkableTileInRoom(r.x, r.y, ↵
r.w, r.h)

if (!dungeon.player) {
    dungeon.player = new classes.Elf(p.x, p.y)
} else {
    dungeon.player.x = p.x
    dungeon.player.y = p.y
    dungeon.player.refresh()
    dungeon.initializeEntity(dungeon.player)
}
tm.addEntity(dungeon.player)
```

It is important to notice the final if clause though. It double checks to see if the player has been initialized or not. In the case of a scene restart, the dungeon.player value will already be set with an instance of one of our hero classes. If that is the case, instead of instantiating a new hero, we just position the hero we already have and add them to the level with initializeEntity. Calling refresh before the create function ends is important so that at the new level the player starts with all their movement and action points.

During scene restarts, the camera.worldView values are set to zero because the scene is not yet rendered. Because of that, our camera.setBounds code needs refactoring or we'll break the camera when the player moves through the levels.

```
camera.setBounds(0, 0, this.game.config.width, ↩
this.game.config.height)
```

We must add a dungeon-changed listener to the UI scene as well.

Changing the UI scene

Only one change is needed at this file, and it is the aforementioned custom event handler. Let's add it to the top of the create function just like we did for the world scene.

```
create: function () {
    console.log("create ui")
    this.createdUI = false

    this.scene.get('world-scene').events.once( ↩
    'dungeon-changed', () => {
        this.scene.restart()
    })
```

So far, we've been calling and assuming the existence of many housekeeping functions which we haven't implemented yet. Let's go over them in the next section.

Housekeeping functions

I've been calling them housekeeping functions because they're supposed to tidy up our game state before we do scene restarts. They must be added to many different files, and some are more complex than others, but in this section, we're going to tackle the simpler ones as a single long section so that we can quickly get over them and be back into doing fun stuff.

First, let's make the changes we need to the *turn manager*. We need a way to empty it before restarting the scene so that we don't carry game entities from one level to the other. In turnManager.js, add the following function:

```
cleanup: () => {
    tm.entities.forEach(e => {
        if (e.sprite) {
            e.sprite.destroy()
        }
        if (e.UIsprite) {
            e.UIsprite.destroy()
        }
    })
    tm.removeAllEntities()
}
```

Before using removeAllEntities to reset the entities set back to an empty collection, we need to dispose all the entity sprites. To be honest, I thought originally that this was not needed and that the scene restart would dispose of the sprites, but while implementing the sample for this chapter, I was ending with duplicate sprites on the screen. That bug might have been somewhere else; as I've mentioned before, I assumed the fadeout callback was executed only once, so the duplicated sprites might have been a side effect of multiple callbacks executing there with a slightly different codebase that was my first experiment.

Anyway, I'm being explicit about the challenges and bugs I faced (most of which are my own creation) because we often read books where all the code is perfect and works the first time, and we have this feeling that authors know exactly what is going on all the time and implement perfect code from the start. If any reader devotes more time to think about it, they'll notice that this is actually not only improbable but also impossible; if authors had such command of programming that they could sprout dozens of complex samples per book all perfect and bug-free from their very first lines, then why would we experience bugs in our day-to-day life both as users and as developers? Authors are developers just like the rest of us; they just have the luxury of being able to edit over and over until things look tidy and perfect enough for sharing.

This leads to a potential fantasy mindset in which authors do not err, and in reality, we all do. I had week-long blocks trying to fix stuff on some of these demos because of bugs and misunderstandings; this happens to everyone. As your career in gamedev progresses, or if you're a seasoned game developer, you might agree you'll end up with some code that feels like superstition, doing things in a certain way because it feels or behaves better.

That is why I'm manually disposing of sprites here; doing it the other way caused trouble that I couldn't pinpoint with enough accuracy to work on a fix. Doing it this way feels unnecessary (because the scene restart would dispose them anyway) and wasteful, but it worked, so I've kept it. Probably, if you start studying codebases for popular open source roguelikes, you'll see similar things with comments like *run this routine twice because it works better.* There is no perfect developer, no perfect codebase, no straight path from empty file into award-winning game of the year entry. Being honest about where I, as an author writing samples for a book, experienced challenges will shatter any potential ivory tower wise developer wizard semblance I might have had, but is what is correct to do.

The method behind this book is one of technological experimentation, building a game by working and reworking our source code. Dead ends, challenges, and dealing with bugs are a part of the process.

After that brief detour into a real-world talk about being a developer, it is time to move back into housekeeping routines. The new `initializeEntity` method of the dungeon module calls `entity.setEvents`; we must implement empty functions for it in both `genericItem.js` and `basicEnemy.js`.

```
setEvents() {

}
```

The version of that for the `basicHero` class is a bit more involved, especially since that class needs more work than just adding that function.

A hero that walks through stairs

Two changes are needed in the basicHero.js class. We need to externalize the handling of input into its own `setEvents` function; that is easy, but we also need to work out how the player will interact with stairs.

The constructor has been changed to just set some basic default values for some properties.

```
constructor(x, y) {
    super(x,y)
    this.name = "The Hero"
    this.movementPoints = 1
    this.actionPoints = 1
    this.healthPoints = 30
    this.x = x
    this.y = y
    this.tile = 29
    this.moving = false
```

```
        this.type = "character"
        this.items = []
    }
```

Input handling is now grouped inside the setEvents function.

```
setEvents() {
    dungeon.scene.input.keyboard.addCapture(["SPACE", ↵
    "UP","DOWN","LEFT","RIGHT"])
    dungeon.scene.input.keyboard.on("keyup", (event) => {
        if (!this.over()) {
            this.processInput(event)
        }
        event.stopPropagation()
    });

    dungeon.scene.input.on("pointerup", (event) => {
        if (!this.over()) {
            this.processTouchInput(event)
        }
    });
}
```

Talking about input, let's add two new keyboard shortcuts to process Input. These new commands are not something that you would ship in a finished game; we're adding them to help during development. They'll be keyboard shortcuts to move down or up the dungeon; this way we don't need to play the whole game to figure out if moving between levels is working.

```
        // go down the dungeon
        if (event.key == "d") {
            dungeon.goDown()
            return
        }
```

```
    // go up the dungeon
    if (event.key == "u") {
        dungeon.goUp()
        return
    }
```

Keeping with the game entity paradigm, stairs will just be a new kind of game entity. They'll be placed in the map by the world scene (more on that later), and the player will walk into them much like they do with the other entities. Once they do, we'll move up or down the dungeon depending on the type of stairs. To implement that, we'll need to add one extra if block to the turn function, just after the one that checks to see if the entity is of type item.

```
    // Check if entity at destination is a stair
    if (entity && entity.type == "stairs" ) {
        if (entity.direction == "down") {
            dungeon.goDown()
        } else {
            dungeon.goUp()
        }
    }
```

The dungeon module in its own cleanup function calls a housekeeping function from the basicHero class with the same name. This function will need to loop many properties of the running hero instance and delete all the sprites it finds. This is needed because we're retaining the player between scene restarts, and if we don't delete them, we end up with duplicate sprites on the scene.

```
cleanup() {
    delete this.UIheader
    delete this.UIstatsText
    delete this.UIsprite
```

```
    delete this.UIitems
    delete this.UIscene
    delete this.sprite
    this.items.forEach(i => {
        if (i.UIsprite) {
            delete i.UIsprite
        }
    })
}
```

All those properties will be reinitialized when dungeon.initializeEntity is called, passing dungeon.player during the world scene create function.

With just those changes, you could launch the sample and be able to navigate between levels by pressing the u and d keys, but it wouldn't be much fun. To complete this first demo, we need to place some stairs in the dungeon.

Connecting the levels with stairs

Stairs are game entities but are one of a kind, so instead of giving them their own folder like it happened with the others, we're just going to create stairs.js inside the items/ folder because there is nowhere better to place it. Be aware that we're not adding them to the items.js module; we don't want the getRandomItem function returning stairs all of a sudden.

The main function of the stairs game entity is to occupy a tile on the map and have both a specific stairs type and a direction, which is down or up.

```
import GenericItem from "./genericItem.js"
import dungeon from "../dungeon.js"
```

```
export default class Stairs extends GenericItem {
    constructor(x, y, direction = "down") {
        super(x,y)
        if (direction == "down") {
            this.tile = 195
        } else {
            this.tile = 194
        }
        this.name = "Stairs"
        this.type =  "stairs"
        this.direction = direction

        dungeon.initializeEntity(this)


    }
}
```

As you probably noticed, the constructor is a bit different than the ones used for most of the other game entities. This is just to save us the trouble of creating two different stairs files – one going up and one going down – with this version, we can change the direction of the stairs by passing a different argument in the class initialization.

Computing the stairs positions

The best place to figure out what is the best location for the stairs is in the BSPLevel class. Using the different branches in the BSP tree, it becomes easier to position the downstairs and the upstairs far away from each other. Let's add another line to the BSPLevel constructor.

```
        this.addStairs()
```

Levels don't have any notion about where in the dungeon they're placed, so it is better we compute both the location for up and down staircases. When we patch BSPDungeon to expose the stairs for the current level, we'll make sure it hides one or the other depending if the player is at the top of the dungeon or the bottom.

```
addStairs() {
    // Place stairs down in the room at the
    // right-most tree node.
    let node = this.tree.right
    while (node.right !== false) {
        node = node.right
    }
    let r = node.area.room
    let dx = Phaser.Math.Between(r.x+1, r.x+r.w-1)
    let dy = Phaser.Math.Between(r.y+1, r.y+r.h-1)

    this.down = {
        x: dx,
        y: dy
    }

    // Place stairs up in the room at the
    // left-most tree node.
    node = this.tree.left
    while (node.left !== false) {
        node = node.left
    }
    r = node.area.room
    let ux = Phaser.Math.Between(r.x+1, r.x+r.w-1)
    let uy = Phaser.Math.Between(r.y+1, r.y+r.h-1)
```

```
    this.up = {
        x: ux,
        y: uy
    }
}
```

The code for placing them is very similar to the code we use to position the player in the level. This way, the player will end up in the same room as the staircase leading up as they move downward into the dungeon.

Exposing the stairs in the BSPDungeon class

Adding a getStairs function that returns what staircases are available for the level the player is currently in is enough for our needs.

```
getStairs() {
    let stairs = {}

    if (this.currentLevel < this.levels.length - 1) {
        stairs.down = this.levels[this.currentLevel].down
    }

    if (this.currentLevel > 0) {
        stairs.up = this.levels[this.currentLevel].up
    }
    return stairs
}
```

It is quite crucial to double check if the player is at the top of the dungeon or at its bottom and hide stairs that would lead currentLevel to be set to invalid values.

Exposing stairs in the dungeon module

Avoiding unnecessary direct access to the BSPDungeon instance makes it easier to replace in the future. It is better to add a new property to the dungeon module to expose the stairs instead.

```
this.level = this.dungeon.getCurrentLevel()
this.rooms = this.dungeon.getRooms()
this.tree = this.dungeon.getTree()
this.stairs = this.dungeon.getStairs()
```

Adding stairs to the map

Staircases should be the first entities to be added to the dungeon. To do that, we're going to alter the create function of the world scene. They can be added to the turn manager just after we set the rooms variable.

```
// Add stairs
let stairs = dungeon.stairs
if (stairs.down) {
    tm.addEntity(new Stairs(stairs.down.x, ↵
    stairs.down.y, "down"))
}
if (stairs.up) {
    tm.addEntity(new Stairs(stairs.up.x, ↵
    stairs.up.y, "up"))
}
```

Now you have a multilevel dungeon and can try going up and down either using the keyboard shortcuts we set or, the hard way, by fighting your way toward the stairs.

This concludes the first demo. We now have a traversable dungeon instead of a single level. As you try to reach the fifth floor, you'll notice that this game is completely unbalanced, and it is very easy to die. Because of that, we should change how we handle player death and present them with a nice game over screen.

Creating a game over scene

This new sample is located in `chapter-9/example-2-game-over/`. So far, we have been simply reloading the page to restart the game after displaying a boring alert message; it is time we add a proper *game over* screen.

The new scene will just display Game Over on the center of the screen, with a smaller text below telling the player to press any key to restart the game. Instead of using the boring fonts we have been using, for that scene, we'll use a gorgeous new font called *Doomed*[2] by Jack Oatley. To load the font, we just need a little style added to the `index.html`.

```
<style>
    @font-face {
        font-family: "doomed";
        src: url(assets/doomed.ttf);
        font-weight: bold;
        font-style: normal;
    }

    body {
        font-family: "doomed";
    }
</style>
```

---

[2]Doomed font by Jack Oatley: `www.dafont.com/doomed.font?l[]=10&l[]=1`

294

The font file has been placed in the assets/ folder. Phaser has features to load bitmap fonts, and they work better for the kind of games we're building, but creating such fonts is beyond the scope of this book, so I have opted to use a freely available TrueType font instead.

Browsers only load fonts declared with font-face at the time they are needed to display something. Unfortunately, if we try to use the font with Phaser, we'll end up with a race condition as Phaser is trying to display the text at the same time that the browser is loading the font. To solve that, we'll alter the game initialization in game.js to force the font loading before the game starts.

```
document.fonts.load('10pt "Doomed"').then(() => {
    const game = new Phaser.Game(config)
})
```

A new file is needed to implement the scene; let's call it gameOver.js.

```
const gameOver = {
    key: "game-over-scene",
    active: false,
    preload: function () {

    },
```

There is no need to preload anything on that scene or to add anything to update because there is no animation. Only create has code in it.

```
    create: function () {
        const x = this.cameras.main.worldView.x + ↵
        this.cameras.main.width / 2;
        const y = this.cameras.main.worldView.y + t ↵
        his.cameras.main.height / 2;
        this.add.text(
            x,
```

```
        y,
        "Game Over",
        {
            font: "120px 'Doomed'",
            color: "#cfc6b8"
        }).setOrigin(0.5)

    this.add.text(
        x,
        y+100,
        "Press any key to go into the dungeon again",
        {
            font: "24px 'Doomed'",
            color: "#cfc6b8"
        }).setOrigin(0.5)
```

Using the new *Doomed* font, we're adding two large text entries to the screen positioned at the center and above each other. To handle *pressing any key*, we'll use a simple *input event handler* that reloads the page.

```
    this.input.keyboard.on("keyup", (event) => {
        location.reload()
    })
```

The rest of the file is just boilerplate generic code to finish the JavaScript module and a stub update function.

```
    },
    update: function () {

    }
}

export default gameOver
```

Simply having the scene is not enough though because the game initialization inside game.js doesn't know about it. We need to import it.

```
import gameOver from "./gameover.js"
```

Then add it to the scenes array:

```
scene: [world, ui, gameOver],
```

You might have not noticed but in the game over scene object, the active property is set to false. If it was set to true, and present in this array, it would end up on the screen overlapping with the world and UI scenes.

Previously, the game over routine was self-contained and handled inside the basicHero class. Now, we're going to call a function from the dungeon module there.

```
onDestroy() {
    dungeon.gameOver()
}
```

And implement that function in the dungeon module.

```
gameOver: function () {
    this.ui.scene.stop()
    this.scene.scene.start("game-over-scene");
},
```

The way scene management works in Phaser is described in the Scene and Scene Manager[3] documentation. In our game over function, we're stopping the UI scene that will cause it to shut itself down and be removed from the screen, but we're not doing the same with the world scene

---

[3]Scene Manager documentation: https://photonstorm.github.io/phaser3-docs/Phaser.Scenes.SceneManager.html

because calling `scene.start` from that scene will cause it to stop and be replaced with the game-over-scene. We had to shut down the UI scene manually because we don't want it overlapping with the game over screen after the world scene is replaced.

If you play the game now, and get your character killed, you'll see a really nice game over screen like Figure 9-1.

Figure 9-1. *Game over*

Much better looking than that silly alert, right? To complement this gorgeous game over screen, we'll build an intro screen in the same style in the next section.

Building a game intro screen

The purpose of the game intro screen is to offer the player the opportunity to choose which class of hero they want to play with; when it is ready, it will look like Figure 9-2.

This new scene will be the first to load when the game starts, and it will be its responsibility to launch both the world and the UI scene after the player makes their choice.

Figure 9-2. *Game intro*

Inside chapter-9/example-3-game-intro/, you'll find the files for this new sample. Even though this new scene may look more complex than the game over scene, it requires changing fewer files than our previous sample. A new file called intro.js will host our game intro scene.

```
import classes from "./classes.js"
import dungeon from "./dungeon.js"
```

```
const intro = {
    key: "intro-scene",
    active: true,
    preload: function () {

    },
```

It is necessary to import both classes and dungeon because this scene needs a way to figure out which hero archetypes are available to the player and a way to pass their choice to the dungeon initialization code.

```
    create: function () {
        const x = this.cameras.main.worldView.x + ↵
        this.cameras.main.width / 2;
        const y = this.cameras.main.worldView.y + ↵
        this.cameras.main.height / 2;
        this.add.text(
            x,
            y - 100,
            "Nano Dungeon",
            {
                font: "160px 'Doomed'",
                color: "#cfc6b8"
            }).setOrigin(0.5)

        this.add.text(
            x,
            y + 30,
            "Choose your hero",
            {
                font: "28px 'Doomed'",
                color: "#cfc6b8"
            }).setOrigin(0.5)
```

So far, it is almost a carbon copy of the game over scene with large text centered on the screen. The next part of the code is where we dynamically compute which classes are available and display them on the screen. This is done by examining the keys in the classes object and creating the choices using a loop.

```
let classNames = Object.keys(classes)
for (let h = 0; h < classNames.length; h++) {
    let inc = 50 * h
    this.add.text(
        x,
        y + 80 + inc,
        `${h + 1} - ${classNames[h]}`,
        {
            font: "24px 'Doomed'",
            color: "#cfc6b8"
        }).setOrigin(0.5)
}
```

Handling the player's choice uses code that is similar to the one used in the basicHero class to toggle equipped items, a simple keyup event handler that checks to see if the pressed key was a number. If it was, we try to access the corresponding hero class and set dungeon.hero to be a reference to it. This way, all we need to do in the world scene is pick the class reference from that property when initializing the player for the first time.

```
this.input.keyboard.on("keyup", (event) => {
    let classNames = Object.keys(classes)
    let key = event.key
```

```
    if (!isNaN(Number(key))) {

        let hero = classNames[key - 1]

        if (hero) {
            dungeon.hero = hero
            this.scene.stop()
            this.scene.run("ui-scene")
            this.scene.run("world-scene")
        }
    }
```

After saving a reference to the player's choice, all that is left is stopping the intro scene and starting the game.

```
    })

  },
  update: function () {

  }
}

export default intro
```

And add the rest of the code needed to finish the scene module properly. To complete this example, we need to do a small tweak to the player initialization in the world scene. Up until now, we've been hardcoding which class the player would play; now we're going to pick it from the dungeon.hero property.

```
    if (!dungeon.player) {
        dungeon.player = new classes[dungeon.hero](p.x, ↵
        p.y)
```

```
    } else {
        dungeon.player.x = p.x
        dungeon.player.y = p.y
        dungeon.player.refresh()
        dungeon.initializeEntity(dungeon.player)
    }
    tm.addEntity(dungeon.player)
```

Nano Dungeon feels like a much more complete game sample now, but we're still missing a way to win the game. This is the subject of the next section and sample.

Completing the quest

Instead of hardcoding the winning scenario in our current modules, for this example, we are going to work on a new module just for quest management. It will be simple but easy to experiment with so that you feel encouraged to tweak and create new quests and scenarios yourself. This is the final sample for our game, and the code for it is in chapter-9/example-4-quest/.

The idea behind it is a collection of functions that are executed every time the dungeon.initialize function runs. These functions can inspect basically anything in the game by probing the dungeon module itself and add or remove entities to the game. In essence, this is not really a quest module; it is actually more similar to our tag system, a collection of functions that are executed for every dungeon level.

For *Nano Dungeon*, the objective will be to pick the Amulet of Nano Dungeon that is located in the deepest level of the dungeon. Picking that item will instantly complete the game. That is a bit lame I know, but it is a winning scenario and is easy to understand, implement, and tinker with.

Quest complete scene

Since we have been implementing new screens for the past two samples, let's begin this new one by implementing the *quest completed* scene. It is just a variation of the *game over scene*, same code but different text. The code for it is in questComplete.js.

```
const questComplete = {
    key: "quest-complete-scene",
    active: false,
    preload: function () {

    },
    create: function () {
        const x = this.cameras.main.worldView.x + ↵
        this.cameras.main.width / 2;
        const y = this.cameras.main.worldView.y + ↵
        this.cameras.main.height / 2;
        this.add.text(
            x,
            y,
            "Quest Completed",
            {
                font: "120px 'Doomed'",
                color: "#cfc6b8"
            }).setOrigin(0.5)

        this.add.text(
            x,
            y+100,
            "Press any key to go into the dungeon again",
```

```
        {
            font: "24px 'Doomed'",
            color: "#cfc6b8"
        }).setOrigin(0.5)

    this.input.keyboard.on("keyup", (event) => {
        location.reload()
    })

    },
    update: function () {

    }
}
```

```
export default questComplete
```

As with the other ending scene, this one needs to be added to the game initialization by importing it in game.js:

```
import questComplete from "./questComplete.js"
```

and adding it to the scenes array:

```
scene: [intro, world, ui, gameOver, questComplete],
```

That takes care of our winning scenario ending screen. Inside the dungeon module, there is a gameOver function that is used when the player character is killed. A new function called questComplete needs to be created there for when the player wins the game.

```
questComplete: function() {
    this.ui.scene.stop()
    this.scene.scene.start("quest-complete-scene");
},
```

All those changes are analogous to the game over example we've seen earlier. The new stuff comes now that we start implementing the new quest module inside quest.js.

Creating a quest module

Our default quest is to pick the amulet at the bottom of the dungeon, so to effectively implement this, we need to import the amulet item (which we will implement shortly), the dungeon module, and the turn manager.

```
import Amulet from "./items/amulet.js"
import dungeon from "./dungeon.js"
import tm from "./turnManager.js"
```

Quests are just a series of functions that execute for every dungeon level; they can alter the game to insert the necessary items and conditions for a quest to be present. In the scenario we are implementing here, we need a function to add the amulet to the bottom of the dungeon. We know that these quest functions will be executed inside dungeon.initialize for every level, so inside our addAmulet function, we need to figure out if the currentLevel is the deepest level in this dungeon, and if it is, we need to find a place to add the prized amulet.

```
function addAmulet() {
    if (dungeon.dungeon.currentLevel == dungeon.dungeon. ↵
    levels.length - 1) {
        let room = Phaser.Math.RND.weightedPick(dungeon.rooms)
        let pos = dungeon.randomWalkableTileInRoom(room.x, ↵
        room.y, room.w, room.h)
        tm.addEntity(new Amulet(pos.x, pos.y))
        console.log(`amulet added to`, pos)
    }
}
```

306

To make it easier to interact with our quest functions, let's export an array.

```
const quest = [
    addAmulet
]

export default quest
```

Refactoring the dungeon module

Inside the dungeon.js module, import the new quest module:

```
import quest from "./quest.js"
```

Calling the quest functions is just a simple addition to the bottom of the initialize function.

```
quest.forEach(f => f())
```

This will cause all the functions to run for each level that is initialized. This approach is flexible enough to allow you to implement multiple game ending scenarios; I'll give some suggestions later, but for now, let's create the amulet.

Creating the amulet item

The code for the amulet will be in items/amulet.js, but the amulet will not be added to items.js because, like the stairs, we don't want them randomly appearing in the dungeon while we're placing random loot.

Internally, the amulet will work similarly to the cursedGem.js. It will have an actionPoint and a turn implementation; this is so that in every turn that it is in the game, it checks to see if the player got it, and if they do, the amulet will call dungeon.questComplete.

```
import GenericItem from "./genericItem.js"
import dungeon from "../dungeon.js"

export default class Amulet extends GenericItem {
    constructor(x,y) {
        super(x,y)
        this.tile = 942
        this.name = "Amulet"
        this.description = "The Amulet of Nano Dungeon."
        this.actionPoints = 1

        dungeon.initializeEntity(this)

    }
```

The amulet is a pretty blue necklace with pendant item. Using the keyboard shortcuts to go down into the dungeon makes it easier to find it while you are developing the game.

The important code inside it is in the turn function that checks to see if the player has it in the inventory and completes the game if they do.

```
    turn() {
        if (dungeon.player.items.includes(this)) {
            dungeon.questComplete()
        }

        this.actionPoints = 0

    }
```

The remaining code is just boilerplate so that the actionPoints refresh every turn.

```
    refresh() {
        this.actionPoints = 1
    }
```

```
over() {
    return this.actionPoints == 0
}
}
```

The game is complete

We did it! We have implemented a simple casual roguelike from scratch using a non-genre-specific game development library. If you manage to survive the descent into the fifth level, and get the amulet, you'll see a screen like Figure 9-3.

Our game is flexible enough so that it can be extended into a proper roguelike instead of a book sample. There is a working game entity system that allows for the creation of items supporting mechanics that can be as advanced as you want to make them. The tag system permits enemies and items to be assembled from minimal reusable components; extending these with more base monster types and more tags can lead to a very fulfilling experience. Closing up with this new quest module, new winning or losing scenarios can be added to the game simply by creating new items and functions there.

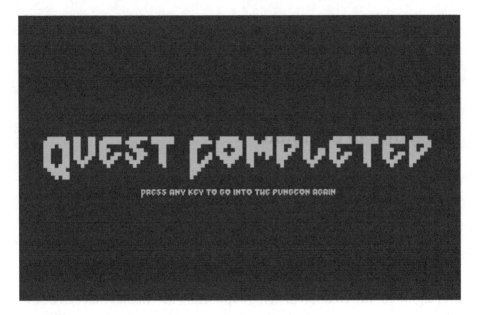

Figure 9-3. *Quest completed*

We must be aware though that *Nano Dungeon* is not a good game; it is a showcase of techniques and experiments on how to create a base, vanilla, casual roguelike. There has been no effort whatsoever into producing a good game design with a story, atmosphere, and cohesive elements. Because this is a book sample, there has been no playtesting to double check for entertainment value and balancing difficulties. Doing games is more than just coding them. There is a lot more involved,[4] and some may say that coding them is the easy part.

---

[4]My favorite game design book is *The Art of Game Design* by Jesse Schell: www.schellgames.com/art-of-game-design/

I'm saying that not to discourage you or to dismiss what has been done in the book. Every learner, in every art form, does a lot of exercises before creating their masterpieces. *Nano Dungeon* is at the same time an exercise and a toolset for doing more exercises. Experimenting with source code is a very rewarding way of learning, and I have tried to make these samples in a way that they are easy to tamper with. *Nano Dungeon* is not the end game, it is the beginning of the journey.

Publishing

Since our game is made of static files, any web server will be able to host it. You can use whatever VPS or shared hosting account you already have to publish it to the Web and make it available to your friends and testers. The steps to do that will vary depending on the hosting. Usually, it is as easy as opening a popular SFTP client and dragging and dropping the files to the server account.

My preferred platform for publishing games is itch.io.[5] They provide free hosting, analytics, forums, and a lot of features for game developers. Once you start making your own roguelikes, I think you really should publish there. Their site has instructions on how to publish HTML5 games to their platform.[6] It can be as easy as uploading a zip with your game files to their website.

If you're already using Node.js for your day-to-day development, there are two companies that are offering solutions for hosting static files that are very popular among people doing small web apps and prototypes. Vercel[7] and Surge[8] are names spoken in many of the

---

[5]Itch.io site: `https://itch.io`

[6]Publishing HTML5 games to itch.io: `https://itch.io/docs/creators/html5`

[7]Vercel site: `https://vercel.com/home`

[8]Surge site: `https://surge.sh/`

trendy web development communities, and many web development boilerplates will come with instructions to deploy apps using those tools. Be aware that both tools offer many more features than what I will outline here, and you should check their websites for more information, to learn their legal terms and service limitations. I think they are a great way to share your games with the world.

Publishing with Vercel

You can install the Vercel npm module globally with

```
npm install --global vercel
```

Then it is just a matter of navigating to the folder where the game is and executing the vercel command from it; vercel will upload everything to their server and give you a URL to access it. Be aware that you need to sign up for a free account with them at their page before you're able to use the tool as it will ask you for a login and password before uploading your assets.

Publishing with Surge

The workflow with Surge is very similar to the one we've seen earlier; you install the Surge npm module globally:

```
npm install --global surge
```

Then using your terminal, navigate to the folder containing the game you want to share and execute the surge command. It will upload all your game files and give you a URL to access it. Like Vercel, you'll need an account at Surge to use their app, but unlike Vercel, you'll be able to sign up for the service from the command-line surge application when you use it for the first time.

Exercises

Now that the game is complete, I'm going to suggest some exercises and changes that require a lot more fiddling in the codebase than simply tweaking some values inside an item. You should have a clear idea how to implement them though as I have been hinting about most of these approaches throughout the book.

- Create a dungeon boss monster and place it near the amulet.

- Alter the quest so that after getting the amulet, the player needs to climb back to the first level and exit the dungeon to win.

- Implement a level progression system that allows the player stats to improve over time.

- Make the enemies more dangerous in deeper levels.

- Create secondary quests that yield powerful magical items at the middle of the dungeon so that the player is better equipped to continue on the main quest.

- Implement a way to drop items from the inventory.

- Add a new scene after the intro that tells a bit of a story leading to the game.

- Enable enemies to use items.

- When the player is going up, the hero character is initialized in the wrong position. They should be placed near the downward stairs. Refactor the code to make the starting position take into account where the player is coming from.

Where to go next?

The next step in your journey is to learn more about roguelikes. There has been much that couldn't be covered here; what we have done is a kick scooter, and there are airplanes out there for you to study and learn from. Roguelikes are a work of love, and many development teams have devoted years and sometimes decades into perfecting and refining their games. It is also a very fun and approachable community. I urge you to

- Check all the amazing articles and games mentioned in RogueBasin,[9] a wonderful treasure trove of roguelike information.

- Watch the amazing videos from Roguelike Celebration,[10] an international conference for people who love the genre, and maybe even attend or present in the future.

- Drop by in the roguelike development subreddit[11] and get involved with the community there.

- Get more books about roguelike development and procedural generation, especially *Procedural Generation in Game Design*[12] which is wonderful.

- Participate and cheer other developers during the 7DRL[13] – seven-day roguelike challenge – an online game jam to create small roguelikes. I might enter a beefied version of *Nano Dungeon* in the next one...

---

[9]RogueBasin site: www.roguebasin.com/index.php?title=Main_Page

[10]Roguelike Celebration: https://roguelike.club/

[11]Roguelike development subreddit: www.reddit.com/r/roguelikedev/

[12]*Procedural Generation in Game Design* book: www.routledge.com/Procedural-Generation-in-Game-Design/Short-Adams/p/book/9781498799195

[13]7DRL challenge site: https://7drl.com/

If your favorite language for game development is JavaScript, check out the roguelike-specific libraries available for it at the RogueBasin site. If you're more interested in the genre than the language, there are libraries for other languages – Rust, Python, Lua, C, C++; there are many options out there – and the techniques you have learned in this book are transferable to other languages and libraries even if the code is not.

This is the start of your journey; you have been given a simple toolset, but even with simple tools, we can build amazing things. I can't wait to see what you'll create with it. Don't be a stranger, and reach out to me with feedback and your own roguelike creations; I'm looking forward to playing your roguelikes.

Index

© Andre Alves Garzia 2020
A. A. Garzia, *Roguelike Development with JavaScript*,
https://doi.org/10.1007/978-1-4842-6059-3

G

H

I

J, K

L

M

N

Printed in the United States
By Bookmasters